MAD MONK
IMPROPER PARABLES
Wit, Wisdom, Humor, Laughter and Practical Advice

Larry Littany Litt

Drawings by
Wonsook Kim

SILVER
HOLLOW
PRESS

To Jung-kwang, who showed me that for outsider artists madness is unavoidable.

Jung-kwang points to the eye of Bodhidharma. "There can be nothing weak about the eye of Dharma, it must be powerful enough to shatter all of our illusions."

from "Mad Monk: Paintings of Unlimited Action" by Jung-kwang, 1979 Lancaster-Miller, Berkeley CA

Front Cover Illustration by Feng Zhou

Larry Littany Litt is a writer and performer who has traveled the globe presenting his stories with music in prose and verse to audiences at art centers, universities and art festivals. He has written articles for dozens for magazines and newspapers on topics ranging from vegan food, spirituality, travel, hiking and mushroom hunting. He earned a Masters Degree in English and Creative Writing from City University of New York.

Wonsook Kim is a painter and sculptor whose work is widely known in Korea and other parts of the world. She has to her credit more than 40 solo exhibitions mounted in New York, Chicago, Los Angeles, Tokyo, Hamburg, Bologna and many other cities. She earned an MFA from Illinois State University.

Website: www.wonsook.com.

CONTENTS

INTRODUCTION

These 60 parables are dedicated to artists, writers and life's travelers who know they are different but carry on boldly because there's nothing else to do. There were and still are many mad monks, not all of them artists. It's a pejorative nickname for an ordained believer who strays from Buddhist behavioral precepts. There are many reasons for breaking with strict religious rules. Main among them is worldly sensual temptation. Some monks can't cope with fighting temptation. Often they just don't want to. They give in. There's no grievous punishment just one's own guilty conscience. And expulsion from the monastery.

Rebellion is an accepted part of religious life. Weren't all the great religious reformers rebels? Monks either leave their order or continue transgressing, pretending they're obeying while they're guiltily enjoying carnal and gustatory pleasures. The latter contradictions and deceptions are where 'mad monkism' begins and resides.

The Mad Monk I knew was born and lived his whole life in South Korea. He was named Jung Kwang, a dedicated believer in Buddhist service to humanity through peace, mindfulness and direct charity. Somehow the Zen precept requiring abstinence from worldly pleasures abandoned him. This didn't make him a bad person in Buddhist thinking. He just strayed once in a while. As long as he didn't disgrace his monastery, life was copacetic. Coexistence is possible.

In 2000 while visiting South Korea for an art event I met Jung Kwang. I was traveling with Nam June Paik, the Korean born philosopher and godfather of video art. We were accompanied by Korean art critic/curator/biennial commissioner Yongwoo Lee, Paik's biographer. They encouraged me to meet Jung Kwang even though he had practically no English and I almost no Korean.

When we met at his mountain studio first thing Mad Monk offered me was a drink from a huge overflowing half gourd taken from a barrel of homemade 'makoli' wine. We toasted "Kumpai!" and drank. Arm in arm he showed me around his studio. We walked out onto the mountain path he traveled daily to his monastery for meals and study.

I mimed and gestured that I liked these mountains, especially the wind deformed trees. He signaled back that this is where his heart sings. We communicated through a universal gestural language about art, music and Nature. I played his Korean drums in my Middle Eastern belly dance style. We drank, he danced. He gave me a copy of his over sized artworks catalog printed in English by one of his wealthy collectors. Before I left his studio he handed me one of his few remaining copies of his long out-of-print poetry book with English translations illustrated with his early ink drawings. It is one of my literary treasures.

Next time I met him was two years later at the GwangJu Art Biennial. He was featured in the traditional ink and brush pavilion. His paintings were far from traditional but they also weren't contemporary by critical standards.

One evening during the biennial I was invited to a collector's dinner party where a dozen traditional painters were lavishly feasted. After a 20 course dinner and much drinking the artists were given the opportunity to paint whatever moved them on a blank unrolled hanji (mulberry paper) scroll.

I was there as a guest. However I happened to have my Jew's harp in my pocket. Unasked, I presumed to play it during this painting performance. While he was painting I was able to imitate the musical sounds of the words 'Jung Kwang.' Yongwoo Lee told me I added to the energy. Many events took place that evening, some very sad others ecstatic. Next day Jung Kwang returned to Seoul and I to New York. He died shortly afterward.

Kwang is the inspiration for these tales. Although these parables aren't directly from his life, they were channeled through Jung Kwang's humane spirit during my convalescence and rehabilitation from both major thoracic and cardiac surgeries. I was in what is colloquially called 'anesthesia amnesia' for two years. I could physically function albeit weakly and slowly. Focusing my mind was difficult. I felt a subtle veil between me and reality. All I could write were poems expressing my limited creative life and my love for walking in the Catskill Mountains.

Suddenly one afternoon in August 2016 while hiking a familiar trail, the mental cloudiness blew away in a gust of pure mountain breeze. I knew I was back. For some still unexplained reason I hung up a drawing of Korea's Buddhist 'sunim' teacher Dalma on my cabin's wall. Then Mad Monk took over. These parables are his channeled journeys on the way to living a full and meaningful though sometimes irreverent creative life.

This book isn't a picaresque novel. Read one parable. Live with Nature. Then read another. Take time to walk, to slowly enjoy your journey. Eat well. Have a drink with friends. See what needs to be done to help your community. Do it. Read another. Enjoy life with Mad Monk.

Main Buddhist Precepts Simplified with some Mad Monk Additions:

For a peaceful compassionate life for yourself and others let go of comparing, lying, competing, judgments, anger, envy, jealousy, regrets, worry, blame, guilt, fear, paranoia, hate and loneliness. Laugh every day especially if laughing about your inability to let go of any or all of these thoughts and actions. Believe you can 'LET GO.' You will know when you've succeeded, when you've failed and when you're faking. Finally you will love all things as they come to you.

The boy who was to become Mad Monk drew pictures from the time he could hold a piece of charcoal. His parents thought it was normal for a quiet sensitive boy. When he went outside to play he took his paper and charcoal instead of a ball. He drew his friends playing games and portraits of everyone around him.

As all parents do they worried about his future. When Mad Monk was 12 years old his parents bade him join them in a serious family discussion. "My son," his mother began, "we have to teach you a skill for your career. I think you would make an excellent butcher like your father. In the future there's money to be made if you open your own butcher shop. There are so many poor people it's easy to get clean up help. The world will always need butchers. In between killing and cutting up animals you can draw and paint."

"With all respect Mother, I don't want to kill animals. Also I'd be at the beck and call of anyone who wants a piece of meat," Mad Monk replied, "I only want to draw and paint."

His mother shrugged her shoulders. Then his Father said, "We want what's best for you, our only son. If you don't want to work in an abattoir you can work with farmers. You can learn how to sow, seed, irrigate, chase away hungry animals and insects, harvest, then take crops to market. Farmers have a good life. In between farm chores you can draw and paint. In winter you can live well in the south like a rich farmer."

Young Mad Monk knew they were thinking about him as only parents do. "What about apprenticing with the village doctor?" he asked, "He has respect. He helps sick people get better. I think I'd like to do that. Plus I can learn to draw different bodies and parts."

His mother was shocked, "That's the same doctor that couldn't help you after you fell on your head from the high branch on the old oak tree. Ever since then all you do is endlessly walk, always drawing pictures. No herbs nor roots nor mushrooms had any effect on you. That changed you. I don't like doctors. All promises offering hope with no results. They gamble with people's lives. It would hurt me terribly if you apprenticed to him."

Little Mad Monk thought for a few long moments then spoke, "Thank you mother, I respect your opinion. Our village lawyer also has much respect. When people need him they pay him lots of money. He has free time to travel. That's what I want. To see and draw the wide world."

"The only people who respect lawyers," his father angrily retorted, "are the ones for whom he's won money and land. The people who hate lawyers are the ones whose money or land he takes for his clients. I'm one who hates lawyers. Because of them we lost our farm to crooked bankers. Lawyers will take anyone's side. They have no loyalty to friends or community. It would shame me if you were a lawyer."

"I'm sorry Father. I didn't know you thought like that. It's time to ponder my future. All I know is I want to draw and paint as much as I can. I'll go for a walk. See you later."

"You can't make a living from painting unless you know rich collectors," said his father emphatically, "which you don't. So get real my boy. Think about your future. When you return we'll talk about this again."

So looking thoughtful for the moment young Mad Monk walked outside carrying his drawing pad, charcoals, ink stick, little stone and brush in his shoulder bag. He walked and walked, wandering right through the village onto the mountain trails. He climbed until he reached the path that leads to the Temple and its monastery. "Why not go there," he thought, "I'm not in a hurry to return home. I know what awaits me."

On the path to the Temple were monks selling 'bujok' good luck charms, Buddhist sutra aphorism posters, monk and nun made handicrafts. Almost in front of the Temple an old monk was selling small portrait paintings of Dalma, the Korean name for Bodhidharma.

Young Mad Monk walked over to the paintings. He stood in front of them staring, following the curved lines and various shadings with his eyes. He'd never seen anything like these ink paintings. The expressions were almost alive. "Do you like what you see?" asked the old monk.

"Yes, I do. Very much. I can see how you did them, but there's something else in them besides lines and shades. I see emotions in the eyes and facial expressions that jump out at you. Each painting is the same yet a different Dalma."

"You can see that?" asked the old monk, "These paintings are some of 1000 Attitudes of Dalma. I am the student of the master 'sunim' teacher who was the student of the 'sunim' all the way through history who first painted all the1000 Attitudes of Dalma. My 'sunim' started painting very young and lived to be very old. He knew more about the 1000 Attitudes than anyone. I hope I will live long enough to paint all the Attitudes."

"Sir Monk, will you allow me to draw one of your paintings," the boy asked excitedly, "I can draw my friend's portraits. This will be something different."

"Ha!" the old monk laughed. "Go ahead and try. To create the soul of an Attitude of Dalma isn't something anyone can do. Especially a boy who isn't even a monk. It took me years to learn to see and paint the Attitudes. And more years to paint them as I see them."

Mad Monk shrugged then sat down in front of a painting. He opened his bag, took out his charcoals, opened his paper book, stared at the painting for a few minutes then began to draw.

The old monk watched him thoughtfully, "Is he the one this curious talkative wandering boy? He knows nothing of monks. So what. Neither did I."

A few minutes later Mad Monk had finished his first drawing. He turned his pad so the old monk could see it. Mad Monk stared at him as he looked at the 'hanji' mulberry paper.

"A very good likeness for a first try with charcoal. But painting is different than drawing. Come to my studio in the monastery tomorrow. Then you can try to paint these with ink and brushes. That's the true test."

"The true test of what?" asked Mad Monk.

"To see if you are the next student of the last master. Who happens to be me. I never found a successor who could paint even one of the 1000 Attitudes to my satisfaction. You can try, but I have very high standards. No one has met them yet. Many have tried. All have failed then gone away disappointed. I tell them they must let go of that feeling. Otherwise they will never be happy."

Mad Monk returned home when it was almost pitch black dark. "Where have you been?" asked his mother. "I made dinner. We waited until we were too hungry to wait any longer. There's some soup, rice and tea by the 'ondol' kitchen stove. Eat first then let's talk."

When Mad Monk had finished his dinner he said, "I must tell you what happened to me today near the Temple. I met an old monk who paints the1000 Attitudes of Dalma. He's invited me to his studio to try to pass his test so I can be his apprentice. If he accepts me I will go into the monastery. I won't need money if I live there. They will feed me and give me a bed."

"Yes they will," said his father, "but you will not be free to be a real man. No sex, no drinking, no business, no hunting or fishing. And no spicy dishes like your mother makes. They are very strict. You won't be happy there. You're still a boy. You don't know the difference."

"As long as I can draw and paint I'll be happy. Besides the old monk hasn't invited me to be his apprentice yet. I will go tomorrow and tell you after."

"I'll never have grandchildren," whined his mother.

"No matter what happens never be a lawyer," his father strongly added.

"Please be a good boy. We want to be proud of you," added his Mother.

Next day Mad Monk went to the old monk's studio in the Temple monastery. "The test is simple," said the old monk, "Paint."

Mad Monk intently painted Dalma's portraits with his own added feelings, expressions and attitudes.

"Ahh yes," observed Master Painting 'Sunim' as he told young Mad Monk to call him, "These are on the way. If you join me here I will teach you to paint so you can sell to the other Temples and wealthy collectors. You must get your parents' consent. You will become a novice monk who obeys the Precepts and Rules. You will live in the monastery. Come here to work every day."

"I'm sure they will allow me to join the monastery. With all respect Painting 'Sunim' may I try to paint my own Dalma portrait now?"

"Go ahead"

Mad Monk painted for a few long minutes. Then he showed his work to his new 'Sunim.' "What is the Attitude?" asked the old monk.

"I call it 'Finding My Career in Spite of My Parents' Opinions.'"

"Too long," said 'Sunim,' "I see it as Dalma contemplating our good fortune at finding our 'Natural Calling.'"

"With all respect 'Sunim,' my father says monks aren't real men. What does he mean?"

"Young man, you can be whatever you want. Don't wear your monk's suit if you do anything that shames the Temple, Precepts or monastery rules."

"Then what's the point of becoming a monk?"

"The monastery is where you can be the painter, sculptor, gardener, woodworker, writer, anything you want that doesn't hurt other people. It's living in the traditions of peace and meditation. Food isn't too bad either. You get used to it."

So Mad Monk joined the Temple as the Painting 'Sunim's' novice. He worked hard to learn how to paint the 1000 Attitudes that would sell. When he was 17 years old he gave his parents one of his paintings. Years later they sold it to a collector. They retired on the payment.

Ten years later Painting 'Sunim' passed on to 1000 Attitudes Heaven. That's when Mad Monk's life exploded with change. He would become the new Painting 'Sunim.' And Mad Monk.

GLASS OF HWADU

Even though he was accepted as a novice to the Painting Master 'Sunim,' Mad Monk knew he must also be tested by Head Monk. If he couldn't give immediate and satisfactory answers to 'hwadu' Chan/Zen koan riddles he would have to move on.

One day shortly after the painting test Mad Monk put on his new monk's suit, walked into San Shin monastery in the verdant forest of beautiful Mt. Mu Dang. He was sent to the Head Monk's office who greeted him coldly. "We have only the most dedicated non-thinkers with the purist hearts living here. They all showed me that they were worthy of acceptance by solving a 'hwadu' riddle to my satisfaction. It doesn't matter to me that the Painting Master 'Sunim' wants you. I make the final decision.

"There is no correct answer," continued Head Monk, "the solution or rather no-solution is up to you. You cannot ask any of our monks or nuns what their answers were. I will know if you did. Your 'hwadu' is this: Is the glass half full or half empty? It's one of the simplest and oldest yet still most important questions for all humanity not only those seeking enlightenment. Though they lived long lives many monks and nuns died never knowing an enlightening answer. There was a hole in their No-Minds."

"Yes Head Monk 'Sunim' I will meditate on this 'hwadu' starting right now. I will soon return to satisfy you. I want to live and work here. I want to be the Painting Master 'Sunim's' novice," replied Mad Monk.

Mad Monk left the Temple walking to the nearby village inn for a meal. He was sitting alone at a small table. Around him older young men were drinking 'makoli' rice wine, telling stories and laughing. Mad Monk couldn't help but hearing.

One of the men loudly said to his friend, "My cup is empty. Kindly fill it up. I will buy the next pitcher."

The other replied, "It's not empty. There's still a drop on the bottom. Empty it first."

The first answered, "A 'makoli' cup is either full or empty. I say this cup is empty. Fill it up."

"Here's the bottle," his friend said, "you can fill it up whenever you want. You had best buy another one when that one is empty."

"This one is half empty already so let's drink until it's done. Then I will buy."

"How do you know it's half empty? Can you see through it? Maybe it's half full?"

"As long as my cup is full I don't care if the bottle's half full or half empty." Mad Monk tapped his forehead. He held in a choking burst of laughter. He stood up, went to where the two loud men were drinking.

"My friends you have enlightened me. You are wise in the ways of 'hwadus.' I thank you. Let me buy you the next pitcher of 'makoli.'" He put down a few coins and left.

The men looked at each other in shock. "This young monk is mad. He pays for a bottle but doesn't drink with us. Next time he's here let's invite him to sit with us. He may buy more pitchers."

The next day Mad Monk went to meet with Head Monk. "'Sunim,' I have my own answer to your 'hwadu.' If it isn't acceptable I will understand that not all answers are. I will leave the monastery and continue to seek."

"It's good and fair that you understand that not all minds are the same," said Head Monk, "in our hearts we must have equal respect for all. Now tell me your solution to the half glass 'hwadu.'"

Mad Monk spoke softly, "The 'hwadu' is an illusion. It is no-thing. I ask a different half glass riddle: is a 'makoli' cup full or empty? If it's empty fill it. If it's full, drink up. When the bottle is empty buy more. Tell stories, laugh and sing with friends. 'Sunim,' that's my solution."

"I think you're quite mad," said Head Monk, "However your commentary on this classic 'hwadu' is the best I've heard. I like you. You are invited to live and work here."

They bowed politely. From that day on the future painter of 1000 Attitudes of Dalma was known as Mad Monk. He still lives and works in the welcoming monastery in the forest on the mountain.

His first painting in his new studio was Dalma contemplating, 'New Answers To Old Riddles.'

EASY MARK

When Mad Monk was still a novice in the monastery, he walked to the village where a famous baker made his favorite sweet rice flour treat, 'songpyeon.' "I love them like I love Nature. All the joys of life are in them. They taste better with each bite," he told himself as he imagined their flavors.

As he walked back to the monastery with his bag of fresh 'songpyeon' a group of young boys around his age dressed in ragged farmer clothes came toward him. As they passed him one of them said loudly, "I smell fresh 'songpyeon.' Yummm!"

Mad Monk thought nothing of it until moments later he was surrounded by the boys. 'Give us some of your 'songpyeon,'" demanded Loud Mouth.

"No, I can't. I'm bringing them back for Head Monk to share with the other monks. I can't return without them."

The boys laughed. "Oh no! Horrors! I can't return without them," they mocked. "Well, we're hungry. We haven't eaten all day. We need 'songpyeon' more than your monks. Monks eat two big meals a day. We poor farm laborers barely eat one if we're lucky."

Mad Monk thought quickly then said, "I will give you some. I will take some with me. That way everybody gets 'songpyeon.' Nobody goes hungry."

"We want them all," demanded Loud Mouth. Give them to us or we'll take them."

As this was happening several older monks came walking along the way going back to the monastery. They saw what was happening. Mad Monk turned from the gang and joined the monks. When he walked a few steps away from the gang he asked the monks to stop for a moment. He reached into his bag. He took out a handful of 'songpyeon.' He walked back to the boys.

"Here's some of what you wanted to take. I'd rather give them then you take them."

The boys were speechless. They looked at him like he was mad. "No need to thank me," said Mad Monk turning to go, "thank the monastery for their generosity."

When Mad Monk returned to the painting studio he told Painting Master 'Sunim' what had happened. "You, my generous novice, must go to the 'tai kwan do' practice yards. You must learn to defend yourself. Poor people think monks are rich. Monks are attacked if they appear weak."

"All I want to do is paint."

"You will paint here in peace. But if you go into the outside world you will meet all kinds of people. Good and bad. Well fed and hungry. We're not supposed to be judgmental. You must learn to defend yourself in case a bad one stares you in the face. Dalma created kung fu for us in China. We Koreans call it 'tai kwan do.' It's what monks do with their hands instead of weapons. You don't want gangs or bandits to call you an Easy Mark. Nothing is worse. Monks must be strong and self reliant."

A year later Mad Monk again walked to the village where the best 'songpyeon' was made. As he returned with his bag full the same gang of boys were there waiting like hawks for any weak looking passersby. "Hey monk, what's in your bag? I smell something very good."

Mad Monk reached into his shoulder bag, "Here are some 'songpyeon' so you aren't thieves today. They're a gift from the monastery."

"We want them all!" screamed Loud Mouth as he rushed menacingly at Mad Monk.

That's when Mad Monk assumed the 'tai kwan do' defense position. "I don't want to hurt you, but I will if you attack me. I have learned that self defense is an attribute of Dalma."

Loud Mouth stopped dead still in his tracks. He looked at his gang, made a gesture to them with his head, took the offered 'songpyeon' then turned and walked away.

Mad Monk walked along the way back to the monastery. When he arrived he handed Head Monk the 'songpyeon.' After supper and sutra lecture the monks each ate one 'songpyeon' treat.

Later that night Mad Monk painted his first personal portrait of the 1000 Attitudes of Dalma, this one contemplating 'Hunger, Self Defense, and Generosity.'

For the next two years Mad Monk traveled the same path bringing extra 'songpyeon' to the gang of boys who by now had respect for him. On the third year the gang of boys awaited Mad Monk. This time Loud Mouth said, "Come with us to the village inn. We drink a little 'makoli.' Others want to meet the mad monk who gives away 'songpyeon.'"

These boys became his trusted village friends. Loud Mouth still wonders if Mad Monk is a 'tai kwan do' expert.

SPICE ISLAND

With a great hunger to experience the world outside his monastery and mountain villages, Mad Monk left his studio in civilian clothes. He filled his shoulder sack full of art supplies. He was headed for the legendary decadent Spice Island. Saying goodbye to Head Monk he walked to the harbor where he boarded a fishing boat to Spice Island. On the way he discovered he loved eating fresh caught grilled fish, a dish he never tasted at his mountain monastery.

When he arrived in Spice City he walked into a famous inn where he ordered the most expensive house special. Lobster, octopus, clams, oysters, shrimp, crabs and mussels were all on the enormous mixed grill seafood platter. He loved every one of these strange creatures grilled to perfection. Every bite brought him closer to Heaven's ecstasy. He ate slowly and savored the tastes with different dipping sauces. His belly was bulging from drinking 'sake' wine. He ate enough for two big monks. When he finally finished his meal he was happy. His curiosity was satisfied. He was sated. He could return home after experiencing new tastes. Now he was a young man of the world.

Then it came time to pay. He dug into his shoulder pack for his wallet. Not there. He turned his pack upside down emptying it on the floor. It definitely wasn't there. The proprietor came over to see what was causing the delay. "Where is your money?" he indicated in the universal money language by rubbing his fingertips together.

Mad Monk replied with a shrug, "I'm a traveling monk from San Shin Mountain monastery on a journey to discover new places and experiences. Your food was excellent. I never had anything like it. Unfortunately I must have left my wallet at home. I'll just go get it. Be right back."

Luckily a Korean trader was at the bar. He translated for Mad Monk and the innkeeper.

"Oh no you don't," roared the innkeeper. "Monks don't eat the way you did. Now pay your bill."

Mad Monk started to slowly back out to the door. Suddenly two men grabbed his arms. "What should we do with him boss?"

"This is a mistake. I'm a monk and painter who has money. In my excitement for travel I forgot my wallet."

"Put him in chains. Throw him in the kitchen," ordered the innkeeper, "let him work 18 hours a day for a few weeks like I do. Then he will know why he must pay."

"Wait," pleaded Mad Monk urgently, "I have something worth more than money. Give me a chance. Please bring a little bowl with water." Mad Monk picked up a sheet of mulberry paper, put it on the table, watered his stone, rubbed his ink, picked up his brush then painted a masterful caricature of the innkeeper as the 'Master of Forbidden Food, Spices and Drinking Pleasures.'

Waiting a few minutes for it to dry, Mad Monk gave it to the innkeeper who studied it carefully then smiled. He showed it around the inn. Everyone liked it. "Okay, you can go. Don't ever come back here without money. Remember this is a business. I don't need two portraits."

When Mad Monk returned to his monastery, he met with the Head Monk. "What did you learn on Spice Island?" Head Monk asked.

"It's a fabulous feast of exotic, delicious forbidden food and wine. But it's not cheap. I had to paint my way out of there. Otherwise today I would be a kitchen slave."

"Your talent served you well this time. But always remember that most business people want money not art."

Mad Monk tapped his forehead. "I believe I learned that enlightenment the hard way. I will always check for my wallet and ask the price before I order."

When Mad Monk returned to his studio he painted Dalma contemplating 'Sometimes Art Is A Meal.'

AT THE ENLIGHTMENT BAR

Because Mad Monk was a curious young man he put on his best street clothes, left the monastery, went to the big city. He walked into a big city bar filled with music and many different kinds of people. He sat on a bar stool looking very sharp and worldly, almost as if he fit in.

An attractive, well-dressed woman sat down on the stool next to him. "I've never seen you here before. Is this your first time?" she asked Mad Monk.

Mad Monk replied, "Yes. I'm trying out the wide world to see if I can fit in."

"How do you like it so far?" she asked.

"Truthfully, I look around and all I see are surfaces," he observed. "Designer clothes, designer hair, designer faces, designer finger nails. Even the bodies look like they're designed to fit into the stylish fashions."

"Are you talking about me?" she asked defensively.

"No of course not. And yes," answered Mad Monk with his usual candid duality. "Because I am talking directly to you I may discover your inner beauty, true inner nature and essence underneath the surfaces you wear."

"And how would you do that?" she asked curiously.

"I will ask you a simple question. Your answer would tell me many things."

"Okay then, ask me."

"What is the sound of one hand clapping?"

She thought for a few moments. She opened her mouth to answer. Suddenly she slapped Mad Monk across his face hard as she could. He fell off his bar stool onto the floor.

"Ah," exclaimed the surprised Mad Monk rubbing his cheek, "You too are the Buddha Consciousness. Thank you for this enlightenment."

She left him there gawking as she sought others who needed less enlightenment.

Mad Monk returned to his studio where he painted Dalma contemplating the 'Difference Between Chan/Zen 'Hwadus' and Dangerous Questions.'

GUILTY PLEASURES

Wandering on the way Mad Monk came upon the Fall Garlic Festival outside the village. The smells of garlic and garlic dishes overwhelmed him. He should have turned around and walked the other way. Instead two things came into his mind simultaneously. First he remembered the Buddhist rules against eating garlic, onions, hot peppers, scallions and shallots. He also remembered his mother's kitchen where those spicy vegetables were used on a daily basis both for delicious flavor and healthy medicine.

He stood paralyzed at the entrance. He knew he shouldn't even think about eating vegetables that are pulled from the ground. That harvesting kills tiny earth bound creatures. Buddhists and other compassionate religion followers are sworn not to kill anything including the lowest of creatures and plants that grow a single food.

Then Mad Monk asked himself, "What are these rules for? What purpose do they serve other than to control my life? I've always loved garlic. I love the stimulation of garlic, how it makes your mouth, throat and stomach come alive while it prevents all kinds of illness. Where do these religious dictates come from? Are they all merely symbolic of pacifism and compassion? Maybe I'm over mindful at this moment. I must think on other things."

Mad Monk then remembered the Head Monk's sermon titled 'Our Sacrifice is Our Badge of Honor.' It was about giving up our former pleasures for Chan/Zen Precepts. How it's our duty, obligation and a reminder that we are an example to all mankind of good, clean and righteous living. Otherwise we would be like the animals in the forest where Nature is a Restaurant.

The Garlic Festival reminded Mad Monk of his family visits to harvest festivals when he was young. He always admired how the farmers would braid the garlic stalks into different shapes. As he stood there reminiscing his craving overwhelmed him.

He ran to his studio put on his street clothes, returned to the festival then tried every variety of garlic, sampled every forbidden dish. First treat he sampled was raw garlic cloves with 'goju jang' pepper paste, 'miso, and a strip of firm 'tubu' Korean tofu wrapped in fresh picked lettuce leaves. "This garlic sandwich," his mother would say, "stops colds and flu all winter. It's better than going to the doctor."

Mad Monk's head radiated delight as he walked around the festival. "Did Dalma do the same as a child?" Mad Monk asked himself, "Did his mother love garlic, cook with it and use it for medicine? Probably not since he came from the West. They don't know what's good."

At dusk when the festival ended Mad Monk returned to his studio, changed his clothes and went to work. Within half an hour Head Monk came in the door adamantly exclaiming, "Know yourself by the temptations you can't resist. Hurt no one but yourself."

"With all respect Head Monk, excuse me," Mad Monk asked, "What are you talking about?"

"Some of our stricter brother monks have complained to me that today you are walking around smelling, no reeking strongly of garlic. They did not commit themselves to this monastery to be assaulted by a forbidden fruit. Not by you or anyone else." Head Monk pulled out a bunch of mint. "Here, eat this herb until you don't smell."

Mad Monk ate the aromatic mint leaves that are usually used for tea. With that Head Monk left without saying good-bye.

The next morning Mad Monk awakened to find some monks reading a note that was tacked to his door. It declared "The Committee on Monk's Conduct is very unhappy with your violation of the Chan/Zen Precept about murder. Because of these many complaints you are therefore fined 28 days of work in the kitchen cleaning pots, pans, bowls, chopsticks and anything else Head Cook wants you to do. If you don't comply we'll take away your studio until you do. Your behavior is a very serious violation. Starting now."

Mad Monk turned to look at the monks who were waiting to see his reaction. He tapped his forehead and said, "Finally I get to work in the kitchen. My mother always thought I should work in food. She will be so pleased that I'm getting a chance to find out what the work is like. This is the best punishment ever."

With that he went back into his studio where he painted Dalma contemplating 'Guilty Pleasures.'

Next day before dawn Mad Monk went to the kitchen to serve his sentence. Head Cook looked at him and said "Please Mad Monk don't get in the middle of my daily meal making routine. I have it under control. Instead paint me a small portrait of Dalma for my room. Don't tell Head Monk."

With that Mad Monk tapped his forehead then ran back to his studio to paint Dalma contemplating 'Punishments Become Pleasures' for Head Cook.

For the next 27 days Mad Monk sat in the kitchen drawing the allowed foods and the variety of dishes they became. On the day 28 he made a book with drawings titled, "Monastery Food Cookbook with Illustrations." Head

Monk had it printed. After many editions it's still for sale in the Temple gift shop.

It was the closest Mad Monk came to working with food. "Even though a book isn't grandchildren I hope my mother will be proud."

TALKING PAINTING

Often as not Mad Monk walked around the monastery grounds speaking loudly to no one but himself. Mornings after breakfast while everyone else was in sutra study he walked to and fro endlessly repeating, "Everything is shit. Shit is everything. Shit is nothing. Nothing is shit. Everything is nothing. Nothing is everything. Shit is everything and nothing. Everything and nothing is shit. My shit is not your shit."

Afternoons during commentaries when the teaching monks talked directly to novices Mad Monk would rant, "Meaning is everything. Meaning is nothing. Nothing is meaning. Everything is meaning. Meaning is meaning. Meaning is a slap inside my head. My head cannot hold meaning. Meaning has fled my head."

In the evenings after dinner during closing sutras and ever more commentary Mad Monk wandered around the monastery grounds loudly declaring, "Everything is everything. Nothing is nothing. The morning is water. The wooden fish is air. Sound is silence. Silence is memory. Memory is the gong. Stream of consciousness is the wooden fish. I reject memory and consciousness. Give me spices, wine and women. The evening is air. Sleep is death. Death is living. The air never sleeps. Death never sleeps. I never sleep."

One day a curious novice followed Mad Monk on his rant walk. When Mad Monk turned the novice was in his face with a question, "Why are you walking around the monastery speaking loudly instead of studying sutras and listening to learned commentaries like the rest of us?"

Mad Monk replied, "Anyone can study and listen. Artists speak from the heart. I have no fear of spices, wine or women. I fear Nothing. However I do fear anyone who wants me to think like them. I serve the true Dalma. Right now I'm walking and talking myself into painting Dalma who speaks Contradictory Truths. My paintings say nothing. They mean everything.

They are the shit that is not shit."

"Do you know that you disturb our prayer and study sessions?"

"Never thought of my preparation for Dalma painting as disturbing anyone. They've never said anything to me. Perhaps the monks can't hear me. Or see me. Or understand my meaning. Or maybe they value my work. My paintings sell very well making lots of money for this monastery."

"If all the monks did as you do there would be chaos," said the novice.

"If all the monks thought like me," replied Mad Monk, "there would be many varieties of beauty in the monastery instead of regimented austerity. Chan/Zen practice is the mind trained not to care about material things or physical beauty. Or sensuality. Or stimulation. Or birth or death. Care about nothing but Chan/Zen No-thingness."

The young monk continued, "I never thought about Chan/Zen like that. I've learned it's about finding and developing my true inner nature and thus enlightenment. Please tell me Mad Monk: If this monastery is such a contradiction to your thinking, why are you living here?"

"Isn't it obvious? A free place to live with studio space, novice interns to clean up after me and pretty good food twice a day," replied Mad Monk with a smile, "I won't find that in the outside world."

The young monk stood there rigid, shocked into sudden enlightenment.

Mad Monk tapped his forehead then ran to his studio where he painted Dalma contemplating 'Something for Nothing That Costs More Than Anything.'

EASILY OFFENDED

While walking along the way Mad Monk saw a young monk sitting on a log. His head and neck were bent forward into his hands almost between his knees. Mad Monk walked towards him. As he came closer he heard the sounds of a young man crying with heaving breaths.

"Excuse me please, "asked Mad Monk, "Why are you crying? It's a beautiful day in paradise on earth. What's your name?"

"I'm crying because my feelings are hurt. My teaching master 'sunim' said I wasn't answering his questions fast enough. I know I'm slow sometimes but I can think right thoughts given a chance. My name is Easily Offended."

"Good name for you. I'm Mad Monk. I'm sure you know that one of the 10 Chan/Zen precepts is to transcend unimportant personal feelings. We must strive for compassion toward all beings and creatures. Your teacher doesn't know he offended you. He has many students to teach. He probably offends them all."

"In my mind I know this precept is right but still my heart is easily offended. I've heard of you. You're called Mad Monk because you don't follow the Tao or Chan/Zen precepts. You say things that are unpopular truths. They say you are also the Master Painter of Dalma portraits."

"True," said Mad Monk, "I never speak falsely even though I may speak in a parable that is not completely thought through. Endings can suddenly change. My life is a contradiction. As long as all beings have not attained Perfection, I simply ask that no one expect me to do so.

"But I'm speaking plainly to you now. Your master has said these same words to me many times," continued Mad Monk, "while I was dreaming of brushstrokes when I should have been thinking of sutras and their many meanings. He didn't make me cry. Instead I thought I'm in my own mindfulness and shouldn't be sitting here listening to young monks answering the same questions day in, day out, year after year. I had other things on my mind. I left off full time studying to do them. That is my story. My advice is be whatever is in your heart and mind. Meditate to discover your true inner nature."

"That's your story. And a good one," whined Easily Offended, "But mine is different. I don't have anything like brushstrokes or paintings on my mind. All I think of is how my mother always told me I am the smartest boy in the world. Even when the teachers told her that I'm not so good in math or geography. I can't remember things. Here in the monastery I'm just a slow boy trying to seek enlightenment from 'hwadus' riddles that aren't coming easily. The riddles are supposed to be a flash of Enlightenment. But not for me. I don't know what to do. Head Monk is going to test me soon. If I can't answer quickly enough I will be sent away." With that he put his head back into his hands.

Mad Monk thought deeply for a few minutes. "I have an idea. Ask Head Monk if you can sweep up in the Assembly Hall after classes. It will give your life purpose. That's all the teachings do. Teaching gives the teacher 'sunims' purpose even though they teach the same lessons over and over again. Let me know what happens."

Several weeks later Mad Monk saw Easily Offended leaning on a broom in the Assembly Hall. He had a satisfied look. Mad Monk went over to him. "Easily Offended you look different."

"Of course. I'm happy now thanks to you. I have found my destiny. My name is changed to Sweeper Up After Wisdom. However Head Monk told me something when he allowed me this job. He said, 'You must keep away from Mad Monk. Next thing he'll tell you is you should have my job.' Was he serious?" asked Sweeper Up After Wisdom, "That's why I haven't come looking for you."

Mad Monk heard this then laughed and tapped his forehead. He ran away to paint the Dalma contemplating 'Good Advice Inspires Laughter.'

USING THE USELESS

"Have you ever asked yourself," asked Head Monk in sutra study, "how do you know you have self worth? Are monks just useless members of society as many productive people think? Are we lazy beggars? Contemplate this question. Come back tomorrow for a discussion on Useful and Useless."

At the next day's study session when it came his turn to speak Mad Monk said, "I'm called mad therefore I'm useless. But also useful as long as people believe in their potential for enlightenment. When they don't believe in sudden enlightenment anymore my work will become useless except to me.

"To me more useless I am," Mad Monk continued, "more spiritual I become. It's my purpose of no worldly purpose that gives me purpose. I don't offer the world food, clothing or shelter. Of what use am I? Yet people want what I create. Somehow the useless becomes the useful.

"IT'S DRIVING ME MAD!" Mad Monk suddenly screamed. "Contradictions! Ever more contradictions! Are they useful or useless? I'm going mad!"

Head Monk forcefully responded, "That's why this monastery exists! We offer peace of mind from worldly and divine contradictions through traditional wisdom with the goal of personal enlightenment and inner peace."

"Thank you for that reminder," said Mad Monk calming down, "I know that wisdom comes from uselessly useful contradictions. The useless is truly useful for me. My painting is useless but not harmful like so many useful things. My paintings are not weapons. They are salves for the mind seeking no-mind."

With that Mad Monk tapped his forehead, stood up and went back to his studio to paint Dalma contemplating 'Useful Uselessness.'

VALUABLE ART

While walking in the village open-air marketplace Mad Monk saw a man carrying a rolled up painting scroll. Since he was always curious about paintings he walked up to him then asked, "My friend, what painting do you have in that scroll?"

"Nothing for you unless you are a collector of famous Buddhist paintings," he replied.

"Then you and I may both have luck today. I am a collector of brush and ink paintings for our Temple. It's the biggest one in this area. Perhaps we will be the next owner of this artwork. What is your name? Let me see please."

"My name is Valuable Art," he said as he unrolled the scroll. When Mad Monk saw it he stepped back in alarm. It was one of his recently finished Dalma portraits.

Mad Monk stared at the scroll and thought, "Valuable Art is holding my painting. He must be a thief. He may be armed and dangerous. What should I do?" He thought a few long moments then said, "From the looks of this painting's developed style you must be a very famous artist. I'd like to buy more than one of your works. Can I come to your studio today? I'm in the market for very good paintings."

"That's not possible," replied Valuable Art, "but certainly I can meet you here tomorrow afternoon with several more scrolls. Be sure to bring lots of money. These paintings aren't cheap copies."

Mad Monk agreed to meet him. He ran back to the monastery where he told some monk friends that a thief was going to rob his paintings that very night. For Mad Monk's protection his friends agreed to stay all night in his studio.

Even though he wasn't supposed to tempt them Mad Monk offered his guests 'makoli' wine. This group of friends drank, sang and finally fell into the unconscious, unmindful, unenlightened sleep of happily sated monks.

In the middle of the night Valuable Art quietly broke into Mad Monk's studio. He lit a candle, looked around, he saw the sleeping, snoring drunk monks. He didn't notice Mad Monk in the darkest corner.

Valuable Art went over to Mad Monk's painting table where several recently painted rolled up scrolls rested. He lifted one up ready to open it. Suddenly a very loud gong rang out from somewhere in the studio. He was surprised and frightened. "I've been caught. I must run," he thought.

He turned to go but no one stirred. So he quickly picked up another one. Again a gong sounded that could awaken the dead. Still no one moved.

Now Valuable Art thought he was free to do whatever he wanted. So he picked up another scroll. This time when the gong sounded all the monks awakened and stood around him. He was surrounded with no escape possible.

Valuable Art looked at the monks then recognized Mad Monk who was holding a gong and mallet in his hand. He blurted, "You! You're the one I'm getting these paintings for. What are you and your friends doing here? I told you not to come to my studio. I should call the police."

Mad Monk was surprised at how clever this thief was. "If you are the master painter you say you are then you can paint a portrait of me right now. Then I will pay you for all these pictures and my portrait."

Valuable Art looked at him and said, "I don't accept commissions. I only sell works inspired by, by…" He couldn't say Dalma because he didn't know what images were on the paintings, "by what I feel from Nature."

Mad Monk looked at him piteously. "We see you squirming in front of us. We know you're a thief not an artist. How? Because these are my paintings! This is my studio. Dalma's spirit directed us to meet in the marketplace."

"What will you do with me? I have children at home. I need to sell something to get money to feed them," begged Valuable Art.

"I will give you money," replied Mad Monk, "if you stay here tonight so I can paint your portrait. I've never met a thief before. I'm trying to understand the combined looks of feigned innocence, masked guilt and defensive cunning on your face when you learned what was happening here. Your expressions were extraordinary and unique. This is a rare opportunity."

"What about me stealing your paintings? Are you going to call the police?" asked Valuable Art.

"No, no police tonight. Instead I'm going to give you a small painting to sell to remind you of the foolishness of stealing and lying.

"Maybe you will let go of your negative thoughts and actions. Maybe you will get a real job to care for your family. Then you will find inner peace."

"I must confess," stated Valuable Art, "I don't have a family. I'm a former monk who steals paintings to spread Dalma's message to the people."

With that Mad Monk tapped his forehead and laughed uproariously. Valuable Art took that moment to grab two scrolls from the table then he ran away.

Mad Monk yelled after him, "I can always paint more paintings but you have only one life. You are wasting it. Give me half the money you get. Then you can steal more of my paintings. We can have a business together."

Valuable Art looked back and shrugged as he ran from the drunken monks toward the marketplace.

The monks opened another bottle of 'makoli' wine, drank and sang until dawn while Mad Monk painted Dalma contemplating "Quick Witted Men Running After Art."

Wearing his street clothes Mad Monk went for a walk in the village. In the village square he saw a poorly dressed man sitting with a big painted sign that read: 'STOP MONKS NOW! PLEASE DONATE.'

There was a bowl for coins in front of him. Mad Monk had to ask, "Stop monks from what? What is your name please?"

"Everyone knows. They're taking over everything. Soon we The People will be forced out of our homes, forced to move to another village, maybe even onto the streets. Until they force us from there too, back into the forest like wild animals. Before long we will live in the shadows. We must stop them. Before it's too late. My name is Sounding Alarms."

"I haven't heard of this. Do you have proof?" asked a puzzled Mad Monk.

"Who needs proof? Look around," said Sounding Alarms. "They're everywhere. Sometimes you can recognize them. Sometimes you can't. Help me in my work. Make a small donation today. And make a regular donation whenever you walk by."

"How will you stop the monks from doing whatever you're afraid of?" asked Mad Monk.

"Oh no, I can't. I'm just the messenger. I can't stop them by myself. Eventually The People will become aware. The People will realize they have to take action. Then they will rise up to stop the monks. Chase the monks out before they chase us. We won't be safe in our homes until they're gone. Don't you agree?"

"I know some monks," answered Mad Monk, "they seem like very nice people. They stay apart from the village in their monastery. They're dedicated to lives of prayer, study, hard work and asceticism. From what I can see they don't want to have anything to do with the outside world."

"That may be what you see," retorted Sounding Alarms vehemently, "but I see a group of men in a private cult waiting to get our money and property because they don't work like the rest of us. When they do they give all their money to their Temples. None of it comes out here to The People. They don't even pay taxes. We pay their taxes. Parasites. Leeches. Enemies of The People. Stop them now before it's too late."

"Do you know any monks?" asked Mad Monk.

"No. And I don't want to. I can't stand to look at them with their shaved heads and funny big grey suits. They all dress alike. They all think alike. They never eat at our inns or roadside bars. They don't kill animals. They don't eat meat. They don't bathe. And worst of all, they don't have sex. What kind of man doesn't have sex. Enemies of The Family. They must be stopped!"

"Sounds like you know them very well," said Mad Monk. 'How do you know so much about them if you can't stand to be near them?"

"I've heard stories about them," said Sounding Alarms, "from people who know people who escaped from their cult. Do you know they buy young boys from their poor parents to work for them for free? The boys can't even send money home to help. What kind of people are these holy men? Horrible and dangerous. We must stop them now!"

Mad Monk looked carefully at this angry man. "I won't give you any money but I will tell you that you will always be welcome at the monastery. Come and see how monks really live. You may discover that monks aren't as horrible as you say. Perhaps you will change your mind. At least you will know something real about them. Bring your hate filled heart and fear filled mind."

"Hate them? Did I say I hate monks? Never! I need them. I'm out here working everyday raising money for my family. Without monks I have nothing to excite donations."

"What? Why monks? I don't understand."

"Why monks? Because they won't fight back," replied Sounding Alarms calmly. "I started this donation business trying to raise money to stop tax collectors. People hate tax collectors. I was doing very well until a certain tax collector accused me of not paying taxes on the money I collected. He had people secretly watching me for months, counting how much I collected. When he confronted me I didn't have any money to pay him. Soldiers took me to debtor's prison. In there I was an unpaid farmer. In freezing winter I swept snow outside. I was assigned to keep the prison's Temple Shrine clean. In there I learned that average workingmen hate monks because they're different. That's when I came up with the idea of stopping monks. Hit the right issue then donations naturally follow. Pretty smart eh?"

"You're a horrible man. If I weren't dedicated to non-violence I'd beat you to within an inch. Instead I'm going to see the tax collector."

With that Mad Monk angrily walked away to find the village tax collector. When he found him he told him the Stop the Monks man wasn't paying taxes.

"Oh yes him again," said the tax collector. "I get complaints about him all the time. I've investigated and discovered he doesn't make enough money to pay taxes. He's one of the poorest people in this village. He lives in disgrace in the poor house. I feel sorry for him."

"He says terrible things about monks that aren't true. He should be stopped."

"Until he says something about the Emperor and his Court," said the tax collector, "there's nothing to be done. We are lucky to have that little bit of freedom."

With that Mad Monk tapped his forehead, "Thank you for this enlightenment."

Mad Monk slowly returned to his studio in the monastery. That night he painted Dalma contemplating the 'Contradictions of Freedom."

Next day Mad Monk wore his monk's suit on his walk. He passed by Sounding Alarms who was still sitting there with his Stop Monks Now sign. Mad Monk walked over to him, made a very small donation. They looked into each other's eyes with new understanding.

NATURAL BEAUTY

While walking on the way after a violent spring rainstorm Mad Monk walked off the traveled road towards one of his favorite hidden streams to view and hear the roaring waterfalls. He knew it would be extraordinary with water raging like bellowing bulls. On a high dry boulder next to the furious water sat a beautiful young woman brushing her hair. She was staring into the swollen rushing stream. As he approached he heard her loudly singing, "Beauty is as beauty does. Take me for what I am."

He approached her calling out, "Excuse me miss. You are singing a strange song I've never heard. Who are you?"

"I'm called Natural Beauty. I'm performing my daily hair brushing ritual. I was singing my mantra to the water. Nothing more than that. Thank you for asking. I'm sorry but I can't talk to you. I'll put us both in danger. Go away."

"Danger? What danger?"

"I'm one of the Emperor's concubines. I snuck out of the Palace to see the raging stream's wildness. I grew up near here. This is one of the secret places we swam naked as children. If I'm caught the guards will have control over my future. If they catch me with a man they will abuse me. You must go right now."

Mad Monk was intrigued by Natural Beauty's pleading voice. "Don't worry. No one can find us here if we don't make a lot of noise. You sound scared. Why don't you run away to the Temple's convent. Many former concubines live there. I'm on my way back there now. Come along with me. I know some nuns who will take you under their protection. Of course you'll have to cut your beautiful hair off. Small price to pay for freedom."

"I could never cut my hair. I want to be beautiful. To be admired. I want to live well. I get to wear glamorous clothes and fabulous jewelry when I'm called to entertain the Emperor's political friends and visiting dignitaries."

"Well," said Mad Monk, "that's a life too. But you're living scared. You can't travel where you want. You can't talk to whom you want. You can't choose to love whom you want. You're practically a slave."

"I'm not a slave," replied Natural Beauty angrily, "I serve our Emperor to help make our country great. Beauty is important. He says he can't abide an ugly country. We must be the most beautiful we can be."

"Our nuns are beautiful in the eyes of Buddha. And monks. They resisted the Emperor. Now they share a simple life with purpose and meaning. The precepts aren't hard to live with. I'll let you in on a secret. You can put on street clothes and a wig to go out in the world to do whatever you desire. Most important, they don't live in fear. And the food's not too bad."

"If I resisted the Emperor and was caught before reaching sanctuary I'd be sent to a military brothel. I'd be a common comfort woman having sex with ten soldiers a day. I think that's a fate worse then death. So I brush my hair, stay beautiful and obey the rules to stay alive. I have meaning and purpose in my own way. Now go away," she demanded.

"How can The Emperor be so cruel to his own subjects?" asked Mad Monk.

"Cruel? Cruel?" said Natural Beauty is a rising tone. "He's not cruel. He offers me the good life. I could live in my village, cooking and cleaning house for my mother-in-law like my not so beautiful friends. I could be working in the rice paddies knee deep in water, my hands rough and back hunched and ruined. He saved me from that fate. I owe him my loyalty and my body when he wants it. Now go away and let me comb my hair in peace. I'm starting to dislike you."

Mad Monk stared at Natural Beauty for a few long moments. "Goodbye. Please remember the convent is always there if you want it. There is an alternative."

"Go! Go!" she screamed at him.

"Shhh! I hear something."

Then from behind the trees three men in palace uniforms ran towards them with swords held out. Mad Monk ran away as fast as he could into the woods. He turned for a second to see them tying Natural Beauty's hands and feet.

"Is her capture all my fault?" he wondered over and over as he ran back onto the path leading to the monastery.

Later that night he calmed himself through meditation. He still felt guilty as he painted Dalma contemplating the 'Sufferings of Beauty.'

Mad Monk walked back to that hidden stream many times hoping he would again see Natural Beauty brushing her hair. Only nature's beauty revealed itself.

Mad Monk was walking around the Temple courtyard loudly exclaiming his usual contradictory expletives.

Head Monk walked up to him demanding, "Stop! Don't you have anything better to do?"

"I'm building up my inner forces to make a painting. I'm seeking inspiration from the Dalma's own words. Soon I will be inspired. I will go to my studio and paint."

"Try meditating quietly on his words," said Head Monk sarcastically, "Right now there's something special I want you to do. Go to the convent orphanage. Look around. Find an appropriate wall for a Dalma Portrait. I'm commissioning you."

"What would children care about a painting of our First Patriarch?" asked Mad Monk, "they know nothing about him."

"They need to start learning as soon as possible. Now do as I ask then come back here. Tell me what you think," countered Head Monk.

Mad Monk walked half a mile to the Orphanage. As he approached he saw children of all ages and sizes playing outside, making loud happy noises.

Suddenly they all went silent when they saw Mad Monk. Perplexed, he walked over to a young nun standing by watching over them. He asked, "Why did the children suddenly silence themselves?"

"Because we've taught them to respect monks as holy men who mustn't be distracted by child's play and silly laughter. Monks are serious and devoted."

"They shouldn't fear monks," said Mad Monk, "We're dedicated people who live by our Temple's precepts, outside of society. At least some of us do. What's your name?" inquired Mad Monk thinking the nun was quite beautiful even without hair. She was attractively tempting in that special delicate way of apparently celibate women. He wondered if she understood his meaning.

"That may be true, but children also should learn respect for their elders. I'm called Questioning Nun. Can I help you with something?" she asked smiling at him.

"Perhaps. I've been commissioned to place a painting of Dalma on the orphanage's wall. Can you show me an appropriate place that will be seen by all? One that will also inspire me?"

"Yes I think so," Questioning Nun said then called over another nun to stand by the door watching the children. They went into the orphanage's Assembly Room where children's classes and meals were offered daily. She pointed to a wall next to the convent's small shrine. "Here's where everyone can see the scowling face of your old man Dalma."

"His face isn't scowling," said Mad Monk, "it's only one of his attitudes. He changes all the time. Mostly he's very unhappy with humanity for its attachment to things, emotions and power. As you know from sutra study."

"Aren't we all looking for something that lifts us to transcendent self knowledge, inner truth, enlightened mind and peace?" asked Questioning Nun.

"Meditation, sutra study and dedication to purpose are the Buddhist way" replied Mad Monk. "What more do you want?"

"I want to know why the village people are so much happier than we nuns."

Avoiding her question Mad Monk said, "This is definitely the right place for my painting. I will return tomorrow for more inspiration. Good bye." With that he turned, walked through the door feeling Questioning Nun's piercing eyes on his back.

That night Mad Monk went to the village inn. As usual his farmer friends were drinking and singing their favorite local songs. Mad Monk ordered a bottle of 'makoli' wine then joined in. When the singing stopped Mad Monk told them about the orphanage. "I wonder what would make the children happy to see monks and not fear Dalma's portrait? Children who have suffered so much in life shouldn't be afraid in their own home."

There was quiet at the table. Then Farmer Wongi spoke, "When I want to make my own children happy I make little toys for them. Or give them sweets from the rice shop. Not too often but enough so they remember they should behave when they see me. Mad Monk, bring them treats, sweets and toys. Say they are gifts from Dalma himself."

"Ahhh!" Mad Monk tapped his forehead, "thank you Wongi for this enlightenment."

Next day Mad Monk went to Han Ah Rheum bakery and bought a bagful of sweet rice treats. He went to the toy maker and bought a bagful of small, carved toys and flutes. He put these into a bigger bag that he carried over his shoulder to the orphanage.

When the children saw Mad Monk coming they immediately went silent. He went over to the closest, knelt down, put down his bag, opened it, reached in and pulled out a rice sweet. "This is for you from Dalma who likes children as much as monks do."

Suddenly all the children ran to Mad Monk. He handed out goodies to every one of them. Then he pulled out a few wood toys and put them on the ground. He gestured to the children to take them. He gave out all the sweets and toys. The nuns were watching as he did this. The children were going wild as children do when treated like children. They were smiling and talking to each other, even sharing.

Questioning Nun came over to him. "What are you doing? The children won't eat dinner. They won't study. They won't behave."

Mad Monk interrupted her. "I don't want them to be afraid of me or my painting. The best way to do that is to show them that monks are generous, that we like children. Then I will know my painting is in the right home. I won't give sweets and toys too often. But I'll come back when the moon calls me."

Questioning Nun looked at him with new eyes. "Come back tonight to show me how the moon calls a painter," she said coyly.

"I'll be here. Can you sneak out?"

"I'll try my best."

With that Mad Monk took his empty bag back to his studio where he painted Dalma contemplating his personal rare inner happiness surrounded by happy children. Mad Monk called it, 'The Ways Children Make Men Wiser.'

Next afternoon he returned to the orphanage with the new painting. Questioning Nun was waiting for him. She helped him hang it. Then she showed him a hidden place in the surrounding forest where they could have privacy.

After dinner Mad Monk went to Questioning Nun's hidden tree grove. He contemplated her beauty and grace until she appeared like a dream in the moonlight. "Children and monks need their pleasures," he mused, "no matter what ascetic old men say. So do women."

"I want to talk about Two Mouths," said Head Monk at this night's sutra session. "I know you can't see them but they are there. For instance there are monks who say they are following the main precept of not killing anything. Yet I know they will eat meat. With one mouth they say one thing. With the other they do something opposite. What do you think of that? Be prepared to discuss Two Mouths tomorrow."

Mad Monk was shocked when he heard this. "I know Head Monk is talking about me. Someone must have told him I went to a village party where I ate grilled 'bul gogi' meat. He's going to make an example of me."

Next night after supper the monks gathered around Head Monk to discuss Two Mouths. "Let me give you an example of Two Mouths: when monks look at nuns trying to picture them with luxurious hair and fine clothes that isn't Two Mouths. Imagination is normal. We can control those thoughts through meditation. However when monks sneak off into the forest with shaven headed nuns on balmy summer nights for whatever pleasures they can get, then say to us and themselves they are still celibate, that's Two Mouths. There's no excusing acts of sexual misconduct according to the precepts. That's just consummated carnal desire plain and simple."

There was total and palpable silence in the Assembly Hall. Monks looked cautiously around them, slyly eyeing other monks wondered if they were suspected or being accused by their brethren.

"My point here is that the lie is the greater sin against the precepts. We're all human. We can easily slip off the ascetic path to purity from temptations if we're not on guard at all times. And who can be that self- protective? I say if you indulge in transgressions then don't lie. Don't be ashamed either. Meditate on your transgressions. Do them for the right reasons. Make sure you satisfy both yourself and those you transgress with. I don't want any frustrated and unhappy monks or nuns wandering around here."

Breathless dead silence filled the hall. Some monks lowered their heads. Some wore sneaky grins. Others had no idea of Head Monk's meaning.

"At least," Mad Monk thought, "he didn't single me out. I wonder if he knows about the nun in the orphanage? I certainly wouldn't tell him."

"From now on," continued Head Monk, "rumors, gossip, canards and fabrications about your brothers and sisters living in this monastery and convent are forbidden. It takes Mind away from seeking enlightenment. You put yourself at the lowest level of consciousness. Do you all understand?"

"Yes, Head Monk," came the reply in almost complete choral unison.

"Good. Now what are your comments?"

"With all respect Head Monk," replied Mad Monk, "I agree with both the Ten Precepts of Righteous Conduct and with the natural desires of monks and nuns who are tempted then indulge in transgressions. That includes gossiping. Perhaps there's a solution. Let's call it the Eleventh Precept. It's simple. Everyone can live up to its right behavior. It simply says, 'Don't ask, don't tell.'"

Everyone looked at Mad Monk and nodded agreement. Head Monk said, "Yes, let's try to hold back those negative thoughts and quiet one of the two mouths."

Then Mad Monk went back to his studio where he painted Dalma contemplating, 'Ironies of Human Nature.'

ACHING ENVY

When returning to his studio from his regular morning walk Mad Monk was surprised to see a young monk sitting in meditation on the path to his front door. Mad Monk stared at him for a few moments then asked, "Sorry to interrupt your meditation. Why are you meditating in this strange place? It's not peaceful with people walking by and talking all day. What's your name?"

"My name is Aching Envy. I'm trying to decide how I should enter 'Sunim' Painting Master Mad Monk's studio. In that building lives and breathes the secret source and power of his paintings. I too want to be a great painter of 1000 Attitudes of Dalma. "I know the real reason he is the great one," continued Aching Envy.

"It came to me in a dream. It's because of this studio's Feng Shui and Heavenly Spirit. Something perfect lives in there. Something different than all other studios. I believe it's a gift from Heaven. A vibrating wave of approval and permission in the presence of all-seeing Dalma himself. Mad Monk goes in there then within an hour comes out with a masterpiece. Every time. I must get in. I need to be in, to bathe in that spiritual force."

"Why don't you just go in," remarked Mad Monk. "I don't think he's in there. Knock on the door. If no answer then just walk in. Find your inspiration. He'll never know."

"Oh, I couldn't do that. If he's in there I'd be embarrassed. I'd run away. If he's not there I'd feel like a burglar stealing his work, his ideas. I can't. I can't."

"In that case," Mad Monk stated dispassionately, "I'll go in with you. Then we can be witnesses for each other. If anyone asks."

"Would you really? Oh thank you brother monk."

The young monk stood up then walked with Mad Monk the very short distance to his studio. Mad Monk knocked on the door asking loudly, "'Sunim' Painting Master Mad Monk are you in there? We're here to see how your studio inspires you. Or whatever it is that pricks and provokes your painting mind." No answer. Mad Monk knocked again. Still no answer. He gently pushed open the lockless wooden door.

Mad Monk led Aching Envy into the small studio. A low table, a sitting cushion, a lamp, some brushes in a wide bamboo stalk cup, ink sticks in a box, a rubbing stone, a bottle of water, scrolls of rice, bamboo and mulberry paper were the only furnishings and supplies. It looked like every other brush and ink painting studio. Even the lacquered mulberry paper skylights were common.

"This is what a studio is supposed to look like," Aching Envy excitedly told Mad Monk, "However I know there's something different, some vital inspiration living in here. I have to find it. I won't leave until I do."

"What if 'Sunim' Mad Monk returns?" asked Mad Monk suspiciously.

"Then I will tell him," replied Aching Envy, "I'm here to be possessed, to be taken, to be inspired by his studio's heavenly essence. When I find it I too will be a master painter of the 1000 Attitudes of Dalma. I will know success and happiness. I want to be like him. Only then will I leave to start my own studio."

"Perhaps the first thing you should do on the path to becoming a master painter is let go of your blind envy. It gets in the way of seeing what's really in front of you. There are no paintings of Dalma titled, 'Contemplating Success From Envy.' Perhaps you should start there."

"Kind monk, I do not understand your teaching. Please leave me alone here. I must meditate until this studio inspires me. I must breath the air. Feel its Heavenly Enlightened Spirit."

With that Mad Monk left his own studio. Days later with the help of several carpenter monks he built another one on the other side of the monastery courtyard. There he continued painting the 1000 Attitudes of Dalma inspired by imperfect humanity.

The first painting Mad Monk made in his new studio was Dalma contemplating 'Unreasonable Envy' with the spirit of Aching Envy as his inspiration.

Since then Mad Monk has had many adventures while walking on the way arm and arm with Dalma and his own imagination.

Many years later Aching Envy the once young, now old and grey haired monk still sat meditating in Mad Monk's original studio. He awaits Heaven to breath the fire of painting inspiration. He was named a saint for his dedication and patience. Also as a reminder to all monks and people that it's possible to choose the wrong path.

POET TREE

While walking in the forest Mad Monk came upon a woodcutter resting on a tree stump staring wistfully into the verdant forest. Mad Monk sat down beside him asking, "What are you doing? What's your name? I'm Mad Monk. I talk to people I don't know."

"The woodcutter replied, "I'm making poetry. My name is Poet Tree."

"Cutting down trees isn't writing poetry," Mad Monk declared.

"I didn't say 'writing' poetry." replied Poet Tree. "With my axe I make poetry possible."

"You surprise me Poet Tree. How does a woodcutter make poetry possible if he doesn't write it himself?" asked Mad Monk.

"I create the Tabula Rasa, the blank space where poetry is immortalized."

"How do you do that?"

With a broad wave of his arm Poet Tree explained, "Trees live in the forest waiting to be cut down. Then they're harvested, transported, lumbered, mulched, pulped, finally made into writing paper books for poets."

"Do poets know you are cutting down trees for them?" asked Mad Monk.

"It doesn't matter. What matters is paper is there when poets want some. I'm beginning the process of providing their written memories so they don't need to hold all their poems in their heads. They can continue creating."

"Is that making poetry?" wondered Mad Monk out loud.

"Making paper is the first step in making poetry last beyond the life of a poet's mind."

"There are so many beautiful trees," extolled Mad Monk, "Dalma must love poetry. Thank you for teaching me that Dalma offers all steps in the making of poetry equal enlightenment."

"When Dalma writes poetry I'm part of it," said Poet Tree.

Mad Monk wept when he realized that although trees are Nature's poetic inspiration some must die for humanity's poetry to live eternally.

Mad Monk returned to his studio where he painted Dalma contemplating 'Sacrifices Nature Makes For Poetry.'

MU OR DUH?

Writer's note: 'Mu' is the negative symbol in Chinese for nothing, not, nothingness, un-, is not, has not, not any, no-thing but not "NO." In The Gateless Gate, an often republished 13th-century collection of Chan/Zen koans/hwadus, the first koan/hwadu is titled, "Chao-shu's Dog." The story goes "A monk asked Chao-shu, the Chinese Chan master, "Has a dog Buddha Nature or not?" Chao-shu answered screaming, 'MU!'"

You try to figure it out. Zen masters and monks have puzzled over it for centuries. Mad Monk's version follows:

A valued Regular Collector came to Mad Monk's studio. Looking long and thoughtfully at the Dalma portrait he wanted to buy he asked, "Does this painting have Buddha nature?"

"Duhhh!" answered Mad Monk gently tapping his forehead.

"What?" replied Regular Collector quickly, "You are supposed to exclaim 'Mu!' like the 'hwadu' of Chao-shu's Dog."

"'Mu' is cow speak," retorted Mad Monk, "these paintings do not have cow nature. They are representations of representations of the 1000 Attitudes of Dalma. Because they also exist as paintings in reality they are also presentations. They are Buddha nature and not."

"Duhhh!" responded Regular Collector.

Mad Monk tapped his forehead again, "Thank you for this enlightenment, my dearest Regular Collector."

After some tea and pastry Mad Monk sold that painting to Regular Collector for a much better price.

SPIRITUAL INNOCENCE

A novice monk was sent to apprentice with Mad Monk. "What's your name my new apprentice?" he asked.

"I'm called Spiritual Innocence because I'm new to monastery life."

"Did they tell you I'm a rice wine drinker, meat eater, lover of garlic, spices and a womanizer? Some even say I have illegitimate children living in the nearby villages.

"Did they also tell you," Mad Monk continued, "that I carouse at inns with working people? Did they tell you the rumors that I am very rich and secretly live in luxury in a mansion ignoring every precept of Chan/Zen ascetic precepts? Some even say I am very poor because I give away my money to the needy. Indeed I'm quite a mystery to those who don't know me."

Spiritual Innocence could only be silent in the face of his new master's questions. Eventually he said, "Whatever I can do to help you. I await your instructions."

In a few days Spiritual Innocence learned how to assist Mad Monk in any and every way. Everyday Mad Monk painted new Attitudes of Dalma. Mostly Spiritual Innocence cleaned up and replaced dirty water with fresh while Mad Monk painted portraits with both refined and wild brushstrokes. For his collectors, fans and connoisseurs each brush stroke was a Heaven inspired enlightenment.

Late every afternoon when he finished painting Mad Monk left his studio with an empty sack thrown over his shoulder. He returned very late each night. He did this in all weathers. If it rained or snowed he wore his cape. But always he wore his monk's straw sandals.

One day a committee of senior monastery monks barged into his studio. "We are distressed by the stories we hear of your drinking and carousing," said the senior of senior monks angrily, "you cast a bad image on our monastery. You take pleasure in negating the precepts of Chan/Zen life. You don't meditate or study sutras. You create chaos and disorder where there must be peace and harmony. We the monastery ethics committee voted today to remove you from our monastery's shelter. You are now on your own to make your way in the crude vulgar world. Good luck and don't look back."

Mad Monk looked at the old monks and asked, "Brother monks would you care to join me for a drink to toast my freedom? I have some very tasty fresh 'makoli' wine."

The monks glowered and stormed out. When he looked around, he saw his apprentice crouched cowering in a dark corner. "What are you still doing here? Shouldn't you be going back to law and order with the old farts?"

"I will go soon enough. However first I have a question: where do you go every afternoon and all night with your empty sack?"

"Good question. I thought you would ask sooner. First I go to the food markets. I buy the last of the day's vegetables, tofu, fruits, mushrooms and nuts. Often the vendors save food for me. Then I carry my full bundle to my old mother's house. She wouldn't eat if I didn't cook for her. I sit with her until she falls asleep. It's what she did for me.

"Afterward I go to the village bar to ask if anyone is hungry. There are very poor peasants living nearby who often don't have enough food for their families. Especially in winter. I have so much wealth from my share of selling Dalma paintings. I believe Dalma asked me to help my friends and neighbors. It's my karma.

"After that I visit a woman whose husband was killed in the war. He was my boyhood friend. She is still very beautiful. She is lonely. She is also very poor. I bring her food so she doesn't have to turn to prostitution. I pay her rent. Now that I'm no longer a monk I can marry her. Does that answer your question?"

"May I stay with you to learn the ways to the two worlds?" asked Spiritual Innocence.

"There is only one world," replied Mad Monk, "With many ways to live. You can combine them until the righteous masters of the 'Only One Right Way' get in your own way. Then you can either live your life or theirs."

"May I also ask if you attained enlightenment while you were here?"

"I was born with enlightenment waiting for the right moment to awaken my mind. When I awoke from the waking dream of meaningless words, of arbitrary logic and duplicity I went walking to try to hear my new self. I discovered I had nothing more to say to me.

"Then floating images of 1000 Attitudes of Dalma flooded my mind. Since then I'm Mad Monk who is removed from the monastery at least once a year. After the first time when nothing happened I never leave my studio. They call me back in a month. They need the money my paintings bring. They like to remind me they are my masters. In name only."

Spiritual Innocence tapped the side of his head. "'Sunim,' Master thank you for this enlightenment. I now understand the oneness of universality in its many existences." Then Spiritual Innocence left for the monastery's evening meal.

Mad Monk decided to paint one last picture for the day before he left on his nightly journey. Dalma contemplating 'Fearlessness in the Face of Authority.'

Then he left to fulfill his karma.

PROFOUNDLY UNPROFOUND

Mad Monk was invited to a local poetry reading at the village inn. When he arrived several old men were sitting on two low benches either side of the only long table. All were wearing variations of white silk traditional 'hanbok' shirts over white woven hemp cloth pants. Each had several sheaves of paper in front of him.

The audience sat nearby on thin cushions at low round tables. Everyone was drinking 'makoli' wine. Mad Monk asked the man seated next to him, "What are we waiting for? Soon I'll be so drunk I won't know if there's a poetry reading or a sutra preaching."

Perhaps he was already too drunk. Certainly his neighbor was. "We are waiting for our friend called Profoundly Unprofound. You will enjoy him if you like to listen to beautiful voices full of emotion."

"What kind of name is that for a friend? Does he know you call him that?" asked surprised Mad Monk.

"Yes of course. He earned his name because he has a skill we all admire and would love to have. He can make a law book sound profoundly emotional. He can move an audience of dead dogs to tears. When he reads to us we are transported on his sonic vocal wings. But when he's finished we realize he had nothing inspiring to say about Nature, Heaven or the Human Spirit. His words don't creep into our hearts with enlightened meaning inspiring soaring elation yearning for more."

When Profoundly Unprofound arrived he sat down with the older men at the center table. The innkeeper called his name first to read. He stood up, cleared his throat then read a poem. His voice was deep forceful yet sensitive, full of the exact right emotions like listening to thunder, gentle rain and breezes. In Mad Monk's mind's ear a rainbow appeared after a Spring storm.

Mad Monk like the rest of the small audience listened enraptured.

When Profoundly Unprofound finished reading Mad Monk realized that indeed he had said nothing revealing of his deepest thoughts. Great music with no meaning like a lullaby. Mad Monk neither learned nor felt anything new except that he too fell under the reader's vocal spell.

"We always let him go first," said Mad Monk's neighbor quietly, "he inspires us not to be shy or self conscious. We all read better when he's here."

After the next readers stood, read and were done for the night everyone continued drinking. Mad Monk walked over to Profoundly Unprofound and asked, "Kind sir, I enjoyed your reading tonight. May I be perfectly honest? I think you know that your poetry doesn't have the visions, ideas or meanings of poetic genius. Yet you come here to read among your friends. Why have you continued to write poetry when you know the audience doesn't think much of it?"

"Oh, I've tried and tried to write deeper, more meaningful poems," responded Profoundly Unprofound, "I've meditated on poetical styles and forms. I thought I understood them. I would sit gazing into space contemplating the universe, awaiting inspiration. But nothing profound leapt from my mind onto the page. I never felt the cold spark become a flame. Still I wrote until I was depleted. Then when I came here to read my poems they sounded like a mishmash of everyone's poems. 'Platitudes Without Attitudes' someone told me."

"You read so well," said Mad Monk, "Why don't you read someone else's poems?"

"Let them read their own poems. Perhaps in time they will learn to read with power and emotion. I believe in my one great ability, my voice. I was a stage actor for many years. I was an empty vessel waiting to be filled with a playwright's brilliance. Besides, it's all been said before by much better poets than me. Now I read my poems in my professional actor's tones. It sounds profound but we all know the inspiration isn't there.

"I love reading aloud," Profoundly Unprofound continued, "as much as I loved acting. I love the listeners' looks of rapt attention during those minutes when meaning and truth don't matter. I've connected to them with my voice. It's my own little enlightenment projected onto the Earth and Heavens. I believe that's why they tolerate my mediocre poems."

Suddenly Profoundly Unprofound laughed loudly and deeply then ordered another drink. "Art can make the best of friends or the worst of enemies," he declared as he raised his cup of 'makoli' wine to toast all his poet friends.

Mad Monk tapped his forehead, then ran back to his studio to paint Dalma contemplating the 'Enlightened Soul's Laughter At Itself.'

NOT THE HEAD MONK

Mad Monk was invited to a convocation for all the monastery monks. They were assembled to elect a new Head Monk who would manage both the Temple and monastery buildings and the monks and nuns future needs. Several monks were nominated. Mad Monk was nominated because he was famous. They all drew straws for speaking turns. Mad Monk would speak last.

One after another the hopeful monks talked about their dedication to Chan/Zen precepts, meditation and study. When Mad Monk's turn came he said, "I will make sure we have clean toilets, good food, warm clothes and strong shoes. We will all work on and in the Temple, monastery and convent buildings to make them stronger, safer and warmer. My one promise today is not to bore you with my religious dedication."

The other nominees were outraged by Mad Monk's rudeness. How dare he mock their speeches? When the votes were counted Mad Monk had won. The crowd cheered.

Mad Monk went up the podium, stared at the assembly then said, "Thank you all for voting for me. I'm so sorry to tell you that I can't be your new Head Monk. I have many things to do and paintings to make. Also I believe we don't need a Head Monk. We must learn to take care of each other. In my humble opinion that's the true work of this Chan/ Zen community.

"I must go to my studio now," continued Mad Monk, "to paint a portrait of Dalma contemplating 'Heaven and Earth Reward Cooperation' before I forget what I just said." With that he left the meeting.

The gathered monks were shocked. No one had ever turned down the exalted position of Head Monk. No one had ever told them they didn't need a supreme master. No one had ever told them they could take care of themselves if they worked together. It went against tradition.

A young monk ran after Mad Monk. When he caught up the young monk asked, "What if we can't get along? What if we can't work together and learn from each other? Chaos will take over. It will be the end of a long history of monks in this monastery."

"My friend, you must let go of fear. Entering the untried and unknown is an exploration of your strength and humanity. Whether you succeed or fail isn't important. That you lived in the world is your real reward. Now go back there and help with the work ahead. Use your Chan/Zen learning. Be practical. Maybe you will be the new Head Monk. If you want."

"Where will you go?"

"After I paint for a while I'll go into the village as I always do to share my version of Chan/Zen with my friends at the inn."

"Why don't you share your teaching with us, the monks who elected you?"

"Because I'm Mad Monk. I drink 'makoli' wine, eat meat, fornicate and howl at the full moon. Who would listen to me?"

The young monk tried to say something more. But Mad Monk tapped his forehead then ran away screaming, "Be your own head monk! Be your own head monk."

After the election debacle, the elderly Head Monk decided to continue managing until he found a suitable replacement.

He never did. He is now over 100. He still lives because he never stops working. Neither does Mad Monk.

DR. EVERYTHING NOTHING

Mad Monk was visiting the monastery doctor's office for his physical check up. The doctor looked in Mad Monk's eyes, ears, nose and throat. He felt the pulse in Mad Monk's wrists, felt his neck, listened to his heart, poked him in the stomach, rapped him on the knees and patted him on the buttocks. When the examination was over the doctor said, "Mad Monk please wait outside until I analyze my readings of your outer and inner self."

Mad Monk waited anxiously. Finally the doctor came for Mad Monk, "We must talk. Please come back into my office."

Mad Monk was nervous. Never before had the doctor asked to see him after an exam. Mad Monk went in, sat down, asked, "Doctor, tell me. What is it? What's wrong with me?"

The doctor replied, "I don't know exactly what it is. It's either something or it's nothing. Either you're okay or you're not okay. In good health or not so good. Either you will live or you won't. Ah, it is the human condition. One thing I know for sure: you will come back or you won't come back."

Confused Mad Monk asked, "Doctor is that your professional diagnosis?"

The doctor replied, "Unfortunately, and I'm sorry to have to tell you this my friend, but yes that's my diagnosis. There's nothing I can do and there's everything I can do. If you want me to do everything I can. If you want me to do nothing I can do that too. If you don't want to come back you don't have to. If you want to come back I will be here waiting. I will always be here waiting for patients who will come back or won't come back. My advice is stay here overnight for observation."

Mad Monk thought for intense minutes. He decided he didn't want to think about a medical problem that might kill him. "Doctor, if I don't have to come back then I won't. Just to make sure I don't have to come back I will stay here to see if I get better or worse. I must know."

The doctor looked at Mad Monk, "Ah, a change for the better we never know. A change for the worse we always expect. I don't want you here if you change for the worse. I only want you here if you change for the better. That makes us both look good."

"If I change for the better why do I want to be here?" asked Mad Monk.

The doctor responded quickly, "Because I need company. I need people. Doctors are lonely. People are afraid of doctors. We give them bad news. People hate to go see doctors. But you, Mad Monk, because you are Mad Monk I can ask you to stay overnight or you can leave. If you decide to stay we will drink fine 'soju' wine, eat very well and I know some nuns who know how to make a man feel very good. Your insurance will pay."

Mad Monk thought for a moment then said, "Doctor you've convinced me something is wrong with me. Therefore I will stay. I will try your therapy tonight. Bring on the 'soju wine.' We will eat like princes. Bring on the nuns for massages and other pleasures. If I'm not cured I will stay another night for more of this important therapy."

"I knew you would understand the intricacies of my treatment of your condition," said the doctor, "And I'm sure you will be an excellent patient."

With that Mad Monk went for a walk. He returned after dusk when all the doctor's patients who didn't arrive and the ones who did had all gone home.

Mad Monk and the doctor went to an exclusive private men's club, ordered 'soju' wine and food, then celebrated by toasting to the good health of everyone knew whether they went to the doctor or not. Later four young nuns who had snuck out of their nunnery for the night joined them for drinking games, jokes, poems, stories, songs and every other pleasure. They drank many bottles of the finest 'soju' wine. The doctor paid the nuns well.

By dawn Mad Monk was so exhausted and hung over that he truly wasn't feeling well. He complained to the doctor who said, "You see Mad Monk my treatment works. You felt fantastic like a healthy young man all night. But now you suffer. That's your problem. You must stay another night for more observation."

Mad Monk answered, "But what about daytime. I feel like an old man with a bad headache, runny eyes and weak limbs. I can't paint."

"Ah, that's another story. I can't cure your day sickness. For that you have to find another doctor. I'm a night treatment doctor. Stay here tonight. I guarantee you will feel better."

With that Mad Monk tapped his forehead. Soon as he did he screamed in pain, "Owww! My head hurts! I feel like Dalma is stepping on it with his big foot."

"Ahhh Mad Monk, I could have told you not to tap your head. I didn't because I wanted to see how serious your daytime malady is. This morning you have heard the extreme sound of one hand clapping on your head. Come back tonight. I can predict you will feel much better."

With that Mad Monk left to recover alone. Later that day he remembered why he hadn't been to the doctor in five years. He thought he might go back in one year if the doctor was still there. Or not.

That night Mad Monk did not go back to the lonely doctor's office. Instead he went to his studio where he painted Dalma contemplating 'Painful Enlightenment from Earthbound Spirits.'

RIGHT SIDE OF DEATH

On a beautiful sunny day Mad Monk was walking through a nearby small village. Passing the Farmers Market he saw the oldest monk he'd ever seen very slowly pulling a small wooden cart full to its top. It was loaded up with small paper packages and many cloth shopping bags.

Mad Monk watched him slowly pull his cart down the road. Looking carefully he guessed that each small package contained only one item.

"Hey young fella," asked Mad Monk in a jocularly friendly tone, "Need some help? I can pull your cart for a while. You're going my way."

"No thanks. Matter of fact today I'm doing pretty damn good. In fact, can't complain at all cause I'm still on the right side of death."

Suddenly Mad Monk realized that all he knew, all he would ever know was walking with him on the right side of his own death. "Thank you for enlightening me master teacher 'sunim.' I hope I live as long as you."

"You will," said the ancient one, "if you keep moving. Never let a lawyer get his hooks into you. Don't be a sitting target. And laugh as much as you can. Those are the truths I learned the hard way. Pass it on."

Mad Monk walked slowly back onto the forest path, weeping tears of joy. When he reached his studio he painted the Attitude of Dalma contemplating "There is No Right Side nor Wrong Side Only the Ever Moving, Ever Changing Side of Life."

To this day Mad Monk is trying to think of a shorter title.

EMPEROR PORTRAIT

In a corner of Mad Monk's studio hangs a portrait of an especially ugly, fat, bald, scar faced old man with a murderous look in his eyes. One day a long time collector stopped by to look at new works. "My friend may I offer you a drink of fresh 'makoli' wine? Our local brew is considered one of the best."

As they drank the collector wandered around the studio. "Who is this nasty looking fellow?" asked the collector finding the repulsive portrait. "Obviously not someone I want to know."

"Don't worry, he's not an Attitude of Dalma," began Mad Monk. "I will tell you the story but you must swear never to tell anyone. It begins when one day a royal messenger traveling with soldiers came to my studio. 'You must appear at the Great Palace for an audience with His Majesty The All Powerful Emperor.' Believe me I was scared because I could think of many tricks I had played on high officials in the past.

"I went there on the appointed day. I entered the Great Palace's Great Hall. I was astounded by it's opulence. It was constructed of the finest woods trimmed in gold and silver. Everything was of royal size displaying majestic power. As I approached the throne I was shocked to find the Emperor never appeared in person but instead sat behind a woven gold mesh screen. I approached on my knees as is the Palace rule. Then a guard told the Emperor I was there in front of the screen.

"Mad Monk," bellowed a voice behind the screen, "you are known by your reputation as the greatest painter of the Attitudes of Dalma. I want my portrait painted. I want to be remembered not just as the All Powerful, All Knowing, All Seeing and All Mighty Emperor. I must also be known throughout eternity as the Emperor of 1000 Attitudes of Wisdom.'"

"I can do this for you," answered Mad Monk trying to stare through the golden screen, "but I have to see you to paint your portrait."

"Impossible," said the Emperor, "this is the challenge I offer you. You must paint me without seeing me. If you can paint great pictures of Dalma who you've never seen, then you can paint a great likeness of me. I want this painting in seven days," the Emperor continued, "I fear my end may be near. My enemies are certainly growing in number. I feel them closing in on me. Come back with the greatest painting you've ever done in seven days or I will have you flogged and flayed eight days from now."

"I left the Great Palace afraid for my life," Mad Monk continued regaling his collector, "completely perplexed and anxious with fear. What did I do to deserve this? How could I paint something I couldn't see? My Dalma paintings are based on studying my Painting Master 'Sunim's' many historic Dalma paintings that came before my own lifetime. I decided to ask the Emperor's subjects about his royal appearance and attitudes. "Can you help me?" I asked people in the streets and cafes, "I'm commissioned to paint a portrait of the Emperor. I don't know what he looks like. He hides behind a woven gold screen. Have you seen him?"

"All but one of them said they wouldn't help me because they had never seen the Emperor. The one man who had seen the Emperor said, 'I'd be tortured and killed if I ever described the Emperor to anyone. Your art isn't important enough for me to give up my life.'

"I went back to my studio to meditate on the problem. However I couldn't concentrate. I imagined myself being flogged and flayed, hung upside down from rafters by heavy rope tied around my ankles. The Emperor's soldiers were beating me as I screamed, "I know the 1000 Attitudes of Dalma but not the 1000 Attitudes of the Emperor.

"Next day I asked Head Monk what to do. 'Paint what you know in your deepest heart of hearts,' he advised, 'put yourself in the hands of Dalma's No-Mind Void. If you don't return from the Great Palace we will know what happened. Of course I hope it doesn't. However you never know with Emperors. Whatever happens know in your heart's mind that it was meant to be in the grand scheme of your lives.'

"He wasn't helpful but spoke truthfully. I went back to my studio. I fasted and stayed awake for five days and nights. Finally on the sixth day I sat at my painting table shaking my head. I had only one idea. If it wasn't what the Emperor wanted, well I'd had a very good life doing what I thought best.

"On the seventh day I entered the Great Palace's Great Hall with a huge scroll under my arm. I approached the Emperor who sat behind the woven gold mesh screen. I was announced. "Let me see the masterpiece you have brought," he commanded.

"I unrolled the scroll in front of the Emperor's screen. The Emperor stood up suddenly leaning over the screen. He looked at it carefully. I saw he was a short, fat, bald, ugly old man with scars and bad skin. He didn't look fierce. To me he looked comical. Like a man failing to overcome his appearance."

"What is this?" screamed the Emperor. "Some kind of Mad Monk joke? You had better have a good explanation for this. Or else the earth will drink your blood."

"Your Royal Majesty," I said weakly, "I have always painted what I saw and felt in my heart. The 1000 Attitudes Dalma are like invisible entities who come to me when I'm holding my brush meditating on their aspects. When I did the same for you I saw the truth of your 1000 Attitudes. I painted a thousand tiny holes in the woven mesh of your gold screen. Each one symbolizes one of your royal attitudes. I can't name them all now. It would take years of study to know you. But if you like I can do that."

"Show your painting to the Royal Court," he ordered, "let's hear from them. They are the ones who will look at it."

"I turned around and showed the portrait. There were many mumbles and nods. Fortunately for my skin no protests were heard.

"After this the Emperor loudly declared, "I, Chao Ving, Eternally Living Emperor and Equal of Dalma of 1000 Attitudes accept your portrait of me as a Royal Acquisition. You will be paid on your way out. Which means get out now."

"I was well paid. I left the Great Palace in a hurry. As I was walking back to my studio a beautifully dressed courtesan in a sedan chair stopped me. She pulled the curtain aside and said, "Mad Monk, thank you from all the Royal Courtesans and Royal Officials. We are grateful to you for not painting a true likeness of the Emperor. None of us can stand to look at him. Some of us have to sleep with him. Others have to obey his cruelty to our people or lose their lives.

"Your painting is another reminder that tyrants can be fooled by artists. I am glad you didn't lose your life. If you ever want me send a message saying 'Mad Monk wants to paint your portrait.' I can sneak out at night. You're not the only one who fools tyrants. Palace rumors whisper that he will die unexpectedly in the next few weeks. Tell no one I spoke to you. Our lives are always in danger from his spies."

"Thank you for stopping me," said Mad Monk gratefully, "I felt the same fear from the minute I was brought into his presence."

"You are very lucky," she said, "the last few painters that tried to paint his portrait were flogged and flayed because they asked his enemies what he looked like. The Emperor fears seeing himself as he really is."

"With that I thanked the courtesan then ran back to my studio to paint a portrait of the horrible little old man I had seen behind the screen. I wanted to remember him as he really was, 'The Ugly Tyrant of 1000 Cursed Attitudes.' His portrait will remind me why I only paint Dalma portraits."

The collector left with a new painting and a story. Mad Monk went for a walk in the forest. He always needed a breath of fresh air after telling the Emperor Portrait story.

A few months later The Emperor was assassinated. His very expensive official portrait disappeared. It may show up on the market some day when an old courtesan needs money. You'll know it by the gold screen.

PERFECTION OF IMPERFECTION

While walking in the meadow in the valley Mad Monk came upon a noticeably physically deformed, hunched over man intensely painting a landscape. Mad Monk quietly came up behind him and watched his accurate stylistic brush strokes. His colors and rendering were uniquely personal. Especially his trees. "I can't paint trees with such simple brush strokes. It must take years of practice," he thought with admiration. Mad Monk was so startled at the contrast between the man's painting and his peculiar body and short legs that he thoughtlessly asked, "You paint natural beauty in its perfection. You are very interesting. What's your name? Do you ever wish you had a perfect body?"

"No. Why should I?" answered the oddly shaped painter, "I do everything everyone else does. I have everything I want. I don't worry about my looks. There's nothing I can do even if I wanted to. I'm called Deformed Perfection."

Mad Monk was puzzled. "Are you saying that deformed people are happier than people who always worry about their looks?"

"I only know about myself," answered Deformed Perfection, "I think more about cleanliness and good grooming than how handsome I am. All I know is it's grand to be alive. And it's much better to live without appearance pressure."

"You're not like most people," continued Mad Monk, "for many people in our society a perfect appearance is the first impression of their status. They want to fit in. Some think their appearance is their path to success. They believe appearances create their status."

"Fortunately no one expects me to conform," responded Deformed Perfection, "Although there is one drawback. Nearly everyone I meet expects me to have unrequited love affairs with incredibly beautiful women who fall in love with my talented beautiful soul. Rubbish and more rubbish! If I want sex I pay for it. It's better and kinkier that way. If you know the right women."

"If you don't mind me asking, do you know deformed women?"

"I've met a few over the years," said Deformed Perfection. "They start out liking me. They almost always think I'm the one for them because I'm similar in some external ways. Pretty soon they whine that they can't understand why I don't share their self-pity. I've been told I'm not empathetic, even flawed.

"Truth is I don't want to hear about women's appearance problems," Deformed Perfection continued, "I tell them life is bigger than that. Nature doesn't care how we look. Nature is the most deformed and divine entity under the Heavens. Nature was here before you and your problems. Nature will be here after you and all of us are gone. Nature doesn't care if you suffer because you don't like your looks. So those self pitying women move on to search for someone who will empathize with them."

"You paint trees with a complex spiritual insight into their deformed outer and inner natures. Is this because you empathize with them, perhaps a little more than those women?" asked Mad Monk.

"Women worry too much about everyone's appearances. As you can see I worry about painting Nature's deformities. Want to know something strange? Not one of the so-called deformed women would let me paint her. True Nature isn't self-conscious. Nature is too busy being alive. I want to be here with the living, dying and resurrecting forces of Nature. I accept myself there."

Suddenly Mad Monk tapped himself on his forehead. "Now I'm enlightened. Thank you." Then Mad Monk ran to his studio to paint Dalma meditating under a perfectly deformed tree contemplating 'Perfection of Imperfection.'

ACTIONLESS ACTION

Mad Monk received a letter from the very old Head Monk of a wealthy Temple complex in a town quite far from his own San Shin Mountain monastery. The old Head Monk offered him a newer, bigger and better studio with running water, more wall space to create bigger paintings, more novices to clean up after him, all the meals he wanted and a trained ox to ride instead of walking. "You will have more time to work. You will live comfortably. We know your eccentric reputation. I assure you respect from all humanity here," wrote the old Head Monk.

Mad Monk went to monastery's Head Monk, told him about the offer then asked for advice. "The old Head Monk of that wealthy Temple is trying to create a legacy for himself by attracting you and other famous artists," said Head Monk after hearing the offer. "He wants people to say he had foresight building studios and charisma attracting artists to live and work there. However I believe community, not facility, better drives creativity and inspiration."

Mad Monk thought for a few minutes then replied, "I don't intend to leave this monastery. Also I'm happy to walk everywhere. It's how I meet people. They tell me their stories. If they need me maybe I can help them. I spend lots of time listening. Some people may think it's a waste. I believe it's walking meditation with stops for compassion and benevolence."

"And I know you need them for inspiration," replied Head Monk. "All is as it's supposed to be."

"Besides," added Mad Monk, "the sad ox doesn't want to carry me around. He's a mighty creature unfortunately bound like a slave to work for men. I don't want to ride him. Better he should pull a plow to feed our people."

Mad Monk sent a message back to the old Head Monk at the wealthy Temple with the big studio offer, "Thanks for thinking of me. But no thanks. I'd rather walk small steps than ride a big ox. Maybe you should walk more too so you can understand the inspiration of walking. Besides you can't bring an ox into an inn for a drink or to a mountaintop to see wildflowers."

When the old Head Monk of the wealthy Temple received Mad Monk's message he thought, "I'm disappointed. Who knew Mad Monk was so disrespectful. One day he will fall into ruin. I will be there to laugh."

The wealthy Temple's old Head Monk died soon afterward. When Mad Monk heard this he immediately painted a portrait of Dalma contemplating 'Disappointment That We Can't Have It All.'

While walking in the forest Mad Monk came upon an old man sitting on a log beside the road. He showed a sour unhappy face with scowling grimace and popping eyes. He was sweating like he had just stopped working in a rice paddy on a hot humid day.

"Are you all right sir?" asked Mad Monk in his usual concerned but friendly manner.

"Yes and no. I'm trying to digest a live snake. Also trying to digest a live frog and a crab. It will take some time."

"Why ever would you eat a live snake, frog or crab? There are better things to eat than that," countered Mad Monk. "We monks are vegans who harm no living creatures. We are blessed by animals. What's your name sir?"

"In fact," said the suffering old man, "I'm a strict vegan myself. I do no harm to animals unless they're trying to kill me. I ate these creatures after listening to an inspiring story. I'm called Swallow Anything."

"What story could cause you to do this terrible thing to animals and yourself?"

"Sit with me for a few minutes while I tell you," asked Swallow Anything. "It all began with a beautiful, virtuous, virginal young nun walking in the forest collecting wild herbs. Suddenly she came upon a huge snake about to swallow a harmless frog. Seeing this violence saddened her even though she knew the Ultimate Truth that Nature is a restaurant. Standing there she emotionally begged the snake to let the frog go free. The snake refused. She pleaded with all her soul again and again. In her passion she declared she would even become his wife if he let the frog live.

"On hearing her offer he let go the frog. The snake rose to his full height looking her over with his intense eyes. His imagination went wild. He licked his snakely lips with his pointy, darting tongue. "When?" he asked.

"Come to my cabin in seven days. I will be ready for you," she told him then ran away.

"By the seventh day," Swallow Anything continued, "she had locked and barred all her cabin's doors and windows. On the seventh night the snake came for her. She hid herself in a trunk. He rapped on the door. No answer. He rapped on her windows. She lay in the trunk quiet as a winter tree. For hours he tried to get in. No answer. Finally he decided no one was home so he left. In the morning she sneaked off to gather firewood thinking he would never return.

"On her way to the forest she met a bent over old man carrying a cage holding a very large live crab. She stared at the trapped animal. "Will you kindly let the crab go free? Can't you feel how it suffers so?" she asked bowing to him. "You will be blessed."

"I am eighty years old," he replied, "I have neither sons nor means to make a living anymore. While walking by the sea I happened to find this crab. I'm very sorry young nun but I cannot set the crab free. It is already promised to someone for a good price."

"The young nun had no money," continued Swallow Anything, "so she took off her nun's robe begging him to sell her the crab for it. "No," he said, "I can't."

Then she removed her skirt. "Please take these for the crab's life. You can sell both for much more than this crab," she pleaded.

"He thought for a moment then agreed to the exchange. She took the caged crab back to her home where she performed a ritual to free the crab's body and spirit. That done she set the crab free outside her door. "Go your own way. Live your own life. Be free," she sang to the crab who was still in shock and didn't move on quickly.

"That night the snake returned. He had learned the lesson of closed doors and windows. This time he climbed onto the roof dropping in through the kitchen chimney.

"During the night the nun heard horrific flailing, scratching and flapping around in her little kitchen. Terrified she hid under her bed covers and prayed. Then suddenly all was quiet as the night should be.

"In the morning she went into the kitchen to find the crab dead on the floor. The snake lay next to it bitten into pieces. She realized the freed crab had stayed nearby. It had climbed up the chimney after the snake.

"She properly and separately buried them. Then she wanted to thank the old man. She searched but he was nowhere to be found. No one knew him. No one had seen him. It was evident to the young nun that he must be an incarnation of Buddha, a 'lohan' who created this miracle for her. She went to the Temple to pray with gratitude and sadness at the lost lives of animals. So ends our story."

Mad Monk looked at Swallow Anything and said. "Venerating all life is the moral way. All your suffering is for nothing. Throw up these creatures if you can. Get their souls out of your body, mind and heart. You are not an animal who can eat creature flesh without consequence and corruption. I still don't understand why you would do this."

"I see I've digested this story's animals very well indeed. You're a good audience. You'll swallow anything if well told," he then laughed wildly.

With that Swallow Anything pulled a cage from behind his back holding a large live crab. He stood up carefully then said, "Thanks for listening to my tale. I must be on my way. There are other defenseless virtuous virgins who must be miraculously saved from snakes by crabs.

"Now, if my exciting story has pleased you Mad Monk would you kindly give an old man a few coins to get his next meal? Telling stories makes me hungry and thirsty."

With that Mad Monk tapped his forehead then bowed, "Thank you story master 'sunim' for this enlightenment." Mad Monk took out his wallet, put a few coins into Swallow Anything's shaking hand.

Then Mad Monk ran back to his studio where he painted Dalma contemplating the 'Price We Pay to Hear Good Stories.'

TEMPLE VIRGIN

Mad Monk loved to travel. When he visited great cities he liked to walk around at night. On this night while walking around Taipei's city center Mad Monk headed for Snake Alley in Night Market. This is the famous street where a man can buy fresh snake or turtle blood drinks and their meats. A specialty is deer penis wine and roasted dried deer penis pieces that can't be found anywhere else.

Special market stalls offered varieties of raw and cooked snake blood delicacies and drinks. Mad Monk watched as an orangutan sitting on a wooden table, wearing a silly naval hat, smashed his powerful fist onto the backs of turtles as they waddled around him. Turtles were continuously put out there by a man in a red outfit. He also wore a silly naval hat. They looked like brothers.

After the orangutan stunned a turtle, a very old man with a long beard picked it up, cut off its head down to the long neck, then cut off its eyes and mouth. All that was left was the neck looking like a stubby bleeding snake. The old man threw the turtle's neck onto a charcoal grill. When it was sizzling hot he removed it, cut it into pieces, put them onto pieces of brown wrapping paper then sold the greasy meat pieces to men waiting around the grill.

Mad Monk went to the table, bought a piece of grilled turtle's neck, quickly ate it with a bit of hot sauce before it went cold. Then he walked around the corner into the Great Tao Temple. There he lit incense, walked around until he found a diviner who read his face and palms predicting his future. He paid her a few coins, lit more incense, put the stick into a vase and then walked through the Great Temple's Gate around the corner to the Street of Heavenly Pleasures on Earth.

On this street he walked by open windows where women with painted faces sat on chairs or leaned against the window frames. All of them showed alluring and flirtatious gazes for the men walking by. A very young woman called to him asking, "Does the wandering monk crave Heaven on Earth? Come in before I get busy."

Mad Monk walked up three steps then entered her room. They stared at each other. Finally she said, "Please kind monk be gentle with me. I'm a virgin who was sold yesterday by my poor country peasant parents. I know nothing of pleasing men or women. Do with me what you will but know you're my first. You will bring me from an innocent girl to full womanhood through the eternal ritual of sexual pain. I beg you to be gentle as you would want for your own beloved sister. It will cost you more for my virginity."

"If I'm paying for sex," said Mad Monk, "and I don't have to, I want an experienced woman not a virgin seeking pity, asking me more money. What's your name?"

"Oh sir how can you say these cruel words to a naïve young girl? I'm called Temple Virgin."

"How? I speak from experience. I visited this brothel last year when you were younger. You told me the same story. In my generosity I paid you more. I came back because now I'm willing to pay for your mother who must know many miraculous tricks. I know she's here. Bring her to me."

Temple Virgin retorted sharply. "I am my mother now. You must pay me to have her."

Mad Monk tapped his forehead. He reached into his pocket for the money he earned painting portraits of Dalma. As he had dreamed for a year he spent that night in unforgettable pleasure with dominant mother and submissive daughter.

Next morning as he was leaving he asked Temple Virgin a question, "What happens when you get older?"

"I will help my daughter become a successful Temple virgin like myself as was my mother. I owe it to the Eternal Tao Masters and the Limitless Buddha who bless all of us."

"We are similar. I paint 1000 Attitudes of Dalma. I give most of the money to our Temple and monastery. I keep some of it for myself as a reward for knowing my worth. Now you have my share in exchange for Heavenly pleasures."

"You are welcome here anytime Mad Monk," said Temple Virgin, "Next time you can make erotic paintings of me that will sell to discreet rich collectors. Many are my visitors. I will introduce you. We will share the money."

With that Mad Monk walked away smiling. When he returned to his studio from his travels he painted Dalma contemplating 'Business Wisdom In Unlikely Places.'

On a beautiful, sunny day Mad Monk was walking on the path when he came upon an old monk holding an open umbrella over his head. "Why are you holding an umbrella on this sunny cloudless day? What's your name 'sunim'?"

"My name is Always Ready. I was in the army for many years. Since I don't have a family I joined the monastery to have a place to live and people to talk to when talking is allowed. I carry this open umbrella so I can be ready for anything. Rain, sun, attacking animals, thieves and most important to disguise my identity. We learn in the military to be prepared. To be on our guard for anything suspicious. To be ready to repel invaders. To help in catastrophes. This umbrella is all those things. I thought I was invisible under it."

"Hmm," thought Mad Monk, "a man's story told by an umbrella. A man's life defined by what he holds over his head, told by what it can do and be for him. This interests me."

"Can I hold your umbrella?" asked Mad Monk, "I may want one just like it in case anything unknown or dangerous comes my way. Which may happen since I wander many paths without knowing what lies ahead. My only defenses are my wits and body. Even though I'm trained in 'tai kwan do' martial arts, a hungry wild beast doesn't know or care. It just wants to feed. I sure I'm a tasty morsel of well fed flesh."

"No," Always Ready assertively responded, "you may not hold my umbrella. Get your own. Bring it with you on walks. Perhaps I can teach you to use it properly. A man's umbrella is sacred to him. It isn't shared. It's a life commitment to security, protection and responsibility. I'm the only one who ever holds my sacred umbrella. It's like a ceremonial hat. I don't share. Sorry but that's the rule I learned in the army. Besides I don't even know your name."

"I'm called Mad Monk. Where can I get such an umbrella that will make me invulnerable?"

"This umbrella is only made by one man," replied Always Ready. "He lives up north. He works in his shed making these umbrellas for military people. Have you been in the army? He won't make one for you unless you have."

"I'm in the army right now. The Heaven sent army of the Tao, the Way and Chan/Zen No-thing. The army that brings wisdom to leaders and enlightens men to their own true nature."

"Ha! That's not an army," laughed Always Ready. "He knows you people. You will turn this military umbrella upside down. Turn it into a basket for bringing wild herbs and mushrooms to poor people's tables. He would never make an umbrella for you."

"Thank you Always Ready for that teaching," said Mad Monk, "However I will go to him and ask if he can make thousands of umbrellas.

Then I will give them to people to use upside down for their own good. It will be a reminder to leaders that weapons aren't the way to win peoples' hearts and loyalty."

"It will take many years to make that many umbrellas for peace and plenty," said Always Ready.

"True. Instead I will order thousands of baskets."

"Also take years."

"Then what can I do to create peace and harmony not enforced by weapons?" asked Mad Monk.

"That's the question of the ages. If you find out the answer please let the rest of the world know."

With that Mad Monk tapped his forehead and ran back to his studio. There he painted Dalma contemplating the 'Eternal Umbrella of Peace For All.' He tacked it onto his studio door.

Next day monks and novices came by asking, "Why is Dalma carrying an umbrella?"

"He's showing what's possible," declared Mad Monk, "if you meditate on the message of this painting. You will create a peaceful mind. No aggression, no ambition, no violence."

When Always Ready saw the umbrella painting he offered to buy it. "Would you buy two," asked Mad Monk, "then give one to the umbrella maker so he knows that umbrellas are not only weapons?"

"Only if you sell me the second one for half price."

TEMPLE CHEF

On a brisk winter afternoon Mad Monk was walking through the village market on the way back to his studio. He was thinking about new ideas for his 1000 Attitudes of Dalma portraits. Suddenly he smelled 'kim chi' the name for many famous Korean pickled vegetable dishes. Then he heard a stall vendor cry out, "Dalma's kim chi! Dalma's kim chi! Eat now for instant enlightenment! Very good price end of day! Dalma's kim chi! End of day very good price! Answer 'hwadu' riddles instantly! Enlightenment kim chi! Heavenly delightenment kim chi! Dalma's kim chi!"

Curious as always Mad Monk walked over to the vendor and asked, "How do you know this is Dalma's kim chi? As a strict Buddhist Dalma didn't eat kim chi. It has forbidden spices and herbs in it. This is very interesting to me. What is your name?"

"My name is Temple Chef. I own the newly opened temple food restaurant in the village. I made my special Dalma kim chi this week. I sell it here so the villagers can taste my food. This kim chi has no garlic or scallions. I know it's not spicy enough but I think people will come to my restaurant once they taste my unique offerings. Also I believe garlic is unforbidden if it's used as a medicine."

"How can you say 'Dalma's kim chi?' Sounds like he ate it."

"In fact he did. Dalma ate our Temple kim chi at my family's roadside inn a thousand years ago. Eating is approval. We have a painting by a monk who was there with him."

"Really? I know something about Buddhist paintings. What was this painter's name?" asked Mad Monk.

"It's so old I can hardly read the chop mark but it looks like his name was Jang Gwong. I'm told he was a very important painter back then. He followed Dalma on his Heaven inspired missionary Journey to the East. Jang Gwong painted Dalma every day to show how he changed over the 1000 day journey. Very few of these paintings still exist. Ours is one."

"I'd love to see it. Where is your restaurant?"

"I'm sorry sir monk but you can't see it. If I open the scroll it will fall apart. That will be the end of it," declared Temple Chef.

"How do you know it's really Dalma eating kim chi?"

"You have to believe me. I'm not a bad person. I come from a good family. I tithe to the Temple. I have my own well behaved family. I donate food to the poor. What more credentials do you need than those?"

"I want to see the old scroll. I want to know it's really old. I want to know who was Jang Gwong."

"I'll tell you what. I'll ask you a 'hwadu' riddle. If you can answer right away then I will take you to see the scroll. But you can't touch it."

"What does a 'hwadu' have to do with it?"

"It's how I can tell if you're enlightened or just want to argue with me. Yes or no?"

"Go ahead, ask me your 'hwadu.'" "When is your face a radish?"

Mad Monk instantly yelled at Temple Chef, "MU!"

They stared into each other's eyes for a moment. Then both men laughed until tears came down their faces. Finally Temple Chef said, "Let's go to my restaurant. I will serve you a meal fit for Dalma."

"What about the painting?" asked Mad Monk.

"If it's touched it will disintegrate immediately. You have to trust me."

They walked to Temple Chef's restaurant where Mad Monk ate the tastiest, most sublime meal he ever had without any of the forbidden foods. Sweet potato noodles in sauce, well cooked grains, flavored 'tubu' tofu, and of course kim chi.

After they had dessert and tea Temple Chef brought out a long wooden box that he carefully opened. In it Mad Monk saw a shallow pile of dust and an old silk ribbon.

"This is all that's left of picturing Dalma's joy and satisfaction after eating my ancestor's food and special kim chi. And my family's story told for countless generations whenever they made kim chi," explained Temple Chef.

Mad Monk left Temple Chef with many bows and thank yous. He gave the serving girl a very big tip. Then he ran back to his studio to paint Dalma digesting and contemplating 'Gratefulness for Well Made Temple Food.'

"I wonder if I can barter this painting for meals."

That's how Mad Monk became a regular customer at Temple Chef's roadside restaurant on the way.

BONSAI SELLER

While walking on the way Mad Monk came upon a woman selling beautifully cultivated and shaped bonsai trees in skillfully handmade, subtly glazed ceramic pots. The trees were obviously old and cared for by an expert. That wasn't unusual in those parts. There were many bonsai sellers. However the sign she displayed on the ground in front of her pots was completely unique. It said, "Payment in Wisdom."

"Well," thought Mad Monk, "I very much admire these bonsai. They are works of art. I'm fairly wise. I'm sure I can take one away for free."

He kneeled to admire the plants and pots. He looked at her and smugly asked, "Which wisdom do you wish, Madame Bonsai Seller?"

"If you ask me that question," she retorted, "you know nothing. Move on. Or pay for my trees with cash from your fat monk pocket."

Mad Monk was shocked. He stood there speechless until he asked, "May I try again?"

"Don't ask stupid questions when you really want something," she countered. "When you let go of thinking you are superior to me, only then are you worthy of my tree."

Mad Monk tapped himself on his forehead. "Of course! You are one of the 36 Hidden Tao Masters. Thank you for this enlightenment."

He then ran to his studio to paint his new understanding of Dalma's Attitude the 'Wisdom of Equals.' Later that day Mad Monk brought the bonsai seller his new painting. Silently he unrolled the scroll. She nodded. Silently she took it. Mad Monk returned to his studio with his precious tree of wisdom. Not a word spoken. They had made the ultimate enlightened exchange. She never appeared on the way again.

HASYA YOGI

Mad Monk was walking around the back of the village shops where the children play. As he approached the playground he heard the sound of wild adult laughter. He walked toward the hilarity. When he came to a small clearing he saw a group of seven people laughing, moving around randomly yet making eye contact. He watched from a distance until the laughing stopped.

Finally the laughers sat down to rest. But no. They started laughing in sitting meditation. In a few minutes they lay down on their backs and laughed more wildly looking at the sky.

Mad Monk was fascinated. It looked like they were having some kind of organized hysteria. He watched so intently he felt like laughing along with them.

When they stopped it wasn't as a group. People ended their laughter whenever they felt spent. When it was all over the group gathered around a single man who looked like he was from the West, probably India. They were thanking him with bows and goodbyes. Mad Monk walked over to him, "I saw your group laughing. It was contagious. I wanted to join in but I didn't want to interrupt. What's so funny? Has some evil magician cast a joke spell on you? What's your name?"

"My name is Hasya Yogi. I'm traveling the world teaching Laughter Yoga and Laughter Meditation. We laugh for no reason. The ancient Indian mystic master 'rishis' left us this method of mental relief and enlightenment as an alternative to silent meditation. Some people can't be silent for very long. I was one of them. I see you are a Chan/Zen monk. What's your name?"

"I'm called Mad Monk. I live and work in my painting studio in the monastery on this mountain. I too can't sit in silence for long so I practice walking meditation. Longer I walk more ideas I get for paintings of the 1000 Attitudes of Dalma."

"Do you know there is a Laughing Dalma legend?" asked Hasya Yogi.

"No," replied Mad Monk, "What is it?"

"Dalma sat facing a blank wall in silent meditation for nine years. When he became enlightened he laughed for seven days straight without stopping. His friends in the monastery asked, 'What has happened? What's so funny? Why are you laughing? Chan/Zen meditation is not a laughing matter. Have you gone insane?'

"Dalma answered them," Hasya Yogi continued, "'I'm laughing because I now know that I've wasted my life seeking enlightenment in silence and isolation. I was searching for my hidden inner truth. But it was always right there in me. I walked thousands of miles over mountains and through valleys, in cities and in countryside ever seeking my own truth. Now after many years of silent meditation I finally know the truth. I was seeking myself. Not an Enlightenment that Voids my Mind. That void comes from what you see now. I'm laughing because I've discovered that when I laugh my Mind goes onto the Void. Longer I laugh more serene I am. I have achieved Bliss at last. I can laugh wherever I am. I am Hasya Chan/Zen. I want you all to laugh with me.'" Some did, some couldn't.

"How is it I never heard this? Our monastery is devoted to Dalma's teachings and silent meditation. I'm the only monk that doesn't follow the Ten Precepts to the letter. That's why they call me Mad Monk."

"Come back here tomorrow. We will laugh like children until we are Enlightened." With that Hasya Yogi walked on his way. Mad Monk tapped his forehead and thought, "I may become a devout monk after all. A Hasya Chan/Zen monk. He ran back to his studio to paint Dalma contemplating the 'Mindless Mindfulness of Laughter.'

Next day Mad Monk returned to the park. He felt peer pressure to laugh. He went along with the others, faking it until it was real. His mind/body couldn't tell the difference.

ARTIST'S CLUB

Mad Monk was sitting at a table in a room whose walls were covered in brush and ink paintings. He was being interviewed by the club's admissions committee even though he was invited to join the new but already exclusive Brush and Ink Club.

"I don't care about joining clubs," he thought, "I won't partake in their activities unless the food is great. Still I should find out why this club already has a lofty reputation. I'll bet they won't let me in."

"Mad Monk," said the head of the membership committee, "you have been approved by unanimous vote. Congratulations and welcome.

"You can stay in our exclusive 'hanok' traditional guesthouse whenever you are in the city. Make reservations at least two weeks before you join us for a stay. We're always busy because we're very reasonably priced. People say we have the best artist's bar around town."

"Sir, what's your name? Aren't you going to ask me questions? Don't you want to see my work?"

"I'm called Head Clubman. I run this artist's club. I make sure we don't get any second class artists in our club. We've searched your background. We're sent a committee to see your works. We've spoken to your Head Monk. I hope you enjoy your stays with us. Now onto to the next applicant."

"I'd like to join the admissions committee. I can sit quietly and watch you interview people."

"Of course. More artists sit over here next to me, more imposing we are. Bring in the next applicant. Take a look at his portfolio," Head Clubman ordered.

Mad Monk watched as a young man walked in and sat down in the applicant's chair. "I'm sorry to report but the Admissions Committee has voted on your application. You're not yet qualified to join. You may try again next year."

"But I've done everything your application asked for. I answered every question. I sent you my resume and dozens of paintings. Please tell me why I wasn't accepted."

"I can't tell you why. It's a secret ballot. You wouldn't want us to break our own rules would you?"

The applicant rose from his seat, turned, then quietly and sadly left the room.

When he was gone Mad Monk asked, "Why was he rejected? I liked him. His work transcends the traditional brush painters with his own modern style. It's what I look for in good contemporary painting. And he seemed like a nice fellow."

"Did you notice how he was dressed? He looks like a Southerner. We're Northerners here. We wouldn't be exclusive if we didn't reject people. Someone has to be rejected. This time it's him. Don't think about it Mad Monk. Be happy you're a member. Only thing left for you to do is give us a painting for the club's very important art collection."

"I would if I could. I make it a rule not to give paintings to anyone who hasn't passed my acceptable collection committee's secret vote. The snobs in this club haven't passed. I don't care how you dress."

With that Mad Monk tapped his head and ran out of the admissions committee and back to his studio to paint Dalma's portrait contemplating, 'Judging On Appearances.'

Mad Monk still wonders what dressing like a Southerner means.

DELAYS AND RUSHES

"The reason for the rush is the delay. Conversely the reason for the delay is the rush." This was one of Mad Monk's favorite aphorisms. It came to be when he was in his studio working on the biggest portrait of the 1000 Attitudes of Dalma he'd ever rendered for the Temple.

It was scheduled to be unveiled during Buddha's May 12 birthday celebration attended by the whole village, monastery, convent and Temple community. Pressure was exploding inside Mad Monk's head. He'd never felt anything like this before. "A work this big," he thought, "requires three artists to get done on time. Not just me alone with the deadline a day away.

"I'm under tremendous stress. I'm not used to it. Why did I take on this enormous painting? Head Monk told me that I was the only one who could paint something spectacular for our Temple. So I said "Yes" not knowing how big 'Yes' was going to be. He always gets what he wants.

"I must get this done," Mad Monk thought in a panic, "and deliver it before the birthday celebration so the Buddhist faithful can see how Head Monk spends their tithing. I need a small break from painting. I'm hungry.

When I return I'll be refreshed and ready to carry on. Just for a few minutes."

Mad Monk put on his street clothes then walked down to the village inn. He knew he could relieve the pressure of intense work there. Some of his farmer friends were sitting at the bar. He ordered a pitcher of 'makoli' wine to share, then ordered 'ban chan,' small plates of food. "This is what I need to re-energize myself," he told them.

Later on after they drank four or five pitchers of 'makoli' the villagers decided they would light torches, go into the forest and play 'samul-nori' percussion folk music. The villagers brought their instruments and of course several more pitchers of 'makoli'. Mad Monk loved the local farmer music. He went along thinking he would stay for a few songs. As you know that's not possible. Once out in the forest, Mad Monk stayed out.

By dawn a friend who was slightly awake shook the others who were fast asleep. After all they were farmers. They had to go into the fields. Except for Mad Monk who awakened with a tremendous hangover from too much 'makoli' wine. He walked back into the village where he had a bowl of hangover curing fish soup, then went on to his studio.

When he walked in he saw the huge half finished painting. He thought, "I have to deliver this tonight to the Temple. I must finish it right now. I'll go down to the river and bathe. The cold water will wake me up then I'll be ready to paint."

When he climbed out of the river he put on his monk's suit, went back to the studio, sat down in front of the painting, picked up his brush, looked at the ink block and immediately put his head down on his folded arms then fell into a deep sleep.

Several hours later a young monk walked into the studio to remind Mad Monk that the afternoon meal was being served. He gently shook Mad Monk's shoulder. When Mad Monk opened his eyes he stared wide-eyed at the unfinished painting. "I'll never get this there on time. Go away. I'm not eating until I finish."

"But sir, this is the last meal of the day. You missed breakfast." "What! What time is it?"

"It's almost five o'clock. When dinner is served."

"May the power of 1000 Attitudes of Dalma help me. I've lost a whole day. Go away. Go now!" Mad Monk shouted.

The rush was on. The very thing he tried to avoid was happening to him. "I paint much better when I'm not rushing," he said aloud.

Mad Monk went to work on the painting like a true madman.

Fortunately he knew where every brush stroke needed to go. He worked all through the evening and into the night. He skipped breakfast. When the next dawn broke over the mountains he could see that he'd finished to the best of his ability. "I can't think about what the Buddhists will say about this rush job. If they don't like it I'll paint them another."

He glued it onto an enormous linen backing, let it dry, then rolled it up. He ran to the Temple. When he arrived there he was surprised to find hundreds of Buddhists celebrating. He found the old Head Monk and asked him, "Isn't the celebration tomorrow?"

"No Mad Monk. Today. You have lost a day somewhere. Where's our painting? Everyone is waiting."

Mad Monk unrolled the scroll. The old Head Monk looked at it thoughtfully. "This is the deepest, most spiritual portrait of 1000 Attitudes of Dalma I've ever seen. It will be our treasure. It will be the great prize of our collection. I will put it on the wall right now. You will be introduced as the painter. I will make a speech. You will celebrate with us. Which of 1000 Attitudes is this?"

"Oh no. More pressure," thought Mad Monk. Then he said carefully, "This is called the Attitude of Dalma who knows the 'Reason for the Delay is the Rush and Conversely the Reason for the Rush is the Delay.'"

Head Monk laughed. "It's good to know oneself. Makes it easier to live."

The next portrait Mad Monk painted was Dalma contemplating 'Procrastination Under Pressure.' It hung in his studio for many years. It may still be there.

FAILED WISDOM

One full moon night Mad Monk was walking on the path back to his studio from the village inn. Suddenly he heard what sounded like a fistfight. He left the path guided by the moon shadows until he came upon a monk slapping, grunting and punching himself all over his face and upper body. Mad Monk watched as the monk fell down, got back up then started all over again like in a real fight. Except that he fought alone with himself.

Mad Monk hurriedly walked towards him. As he got closer he yelled, "Stop! You're going to hurt yourself! This is madness. Stop!"

The wildly punching monk yelled back, "There is no truth but the truth you bring to truth. Heavenly Enlightenment avoids me. Disillusioned illusion stalks me. No inner wisdom binds me together. I face ever more lurking failure and self mocking."

"There's no failure if you still seek wisdom," said Mad Monk. "Failure is the gatekeeper of feeling. True failure awakens the seeker. What's your name?"

"My name is Failed Wisdom. The question is: which road do I take after failure? There are so many."

"The answer is within your mind and heart," said Mad Monk. "Some seekers try many paths. Some need only one. We end up the same place. Ever seeking more moments like the first shock of enlightenment. Like a thrill seeker on downhill ski slopes or a parachutist endlessly gliding in the heavens. Like sexual pleasure. Unlike so many feelings enlightenment is ever fresh and vital. If you seek enlightenment with truth and honesty it is always attainable and renewable."

"Intellectually I know," said Failed Wisdom, "that enlightenment often comes as a sudden surprise without warning. I welcome it. I want to be electrified. However I can't coax enlightenment to land its lightning bolts on me."

"Enlightenment is not only knowing the fullness of your own inner nature," replied Mad Monk, "enlightenment is feeling those surges through your mind and body becoming one whole truth with the universe like a shock without falling off a mountain. Like being struck by a powerful wave you can see and feel but can't hold. Like back arching, screaming, laughing orgasms when you don't care about the neighbors hearing yet know they are listening enviously," mused Mad Monk.

Failed Wisdom listened then spoke, "I thought enlightenment was being totally aware of yourself in the universe, knowing your universe is aware of you too. Our enlightened masters say it's a triangular affair with wisdom, compassion and love surrounding you. I tried meditation for three years. Nothing happened. Nothing but noisy thoughts and carnal desires floating through my mind. Then two years later I learned to stop my thoughts and still nothing. Nothing. Nothing. Nothing.

"I'm not going to attain enlightenment like other monks," continued Failed Wisdom, "I should go back to law school. But first I will beat myself into a new person. End this monastic life with a sore body and failed spiritual mind. But I fear the next life with memories of my failure. I will beat it out of my mind." He started slapping himself on his head again.

"Stop! Wait! Hold it!" cried Mad Monk loudly. "Consider yourself lucky to have those moments of mental quiet and peace of mind when you could hear yourself not thinking. Most people never know the sound of silencing their chattering monkeys. For most of us dedicated seekers that's the first step toward enlightenment. After that comes the sudden shock of finding and knowing your own true self-nature in the ever changing, never changing floating cosmos of eternal reality."

"Are you saying I've had my first enlightenment and didn't know it? That my failure is my success? That my nothing is really something?" asked Failed Wisdom.

"You and I are now one. I will take from you what you have given me. I offer you the wisdom I believe I have," replied Mad Monk.

"Thank you 'sunim' master for this teaching. Now I will bathe in the river of intuition to wash away the pain and suffering I went through on the path to failed yet successful enlightenment."

With those farewells they parted. When Mad Monk went back to his studio he painted Dalma contemplating 'Shock of First Enlightenment, Eternal Desire for More.'

"Perhaps Failed Wisdom will be one of the great masters of the future," thought Mad Monk. "His beating himself up technique to attain wisdom is different than laughter meditation or sudden flashes of shock enlightenment. Almost everyone can do it. I may even try it myself one day."

Then Mad Monk tapped his forehead and said out loud to the no one there, "Nah."

FAMOUS ART TEACHER

Mad Monk was walking through the village when he came upon a well-dressed man sitting at a painting table in the village square. Mad Monk stared at him because next to his table was a sign that stated in big red calligraphy: "Learn To Paint Like Mad Monk. First Lesson Free."

When the teacher noticed Mad Monk he asked in a friendly tone, "Yes sir. Can I help you? I usually don't accept monks as students."

"Who do you take for students? What's your name?"

"You look like an honest man. Just between us, not for anyone else's ears, I specialize in teaching the daughters, wives and mistresses of wealthy merchants and politicians. Only their fathers, husbands and lovers can afford my classes. I'm called Famous Art Teacher," he said conspiratorially.

"I've never seen you here before. Where do you come from?" asked Mad Monk.

"I'm from down south. There's no more art teaching business for me down there. If you know what I mean," winked Famous Art Teacher.

"No, I don't know what you mean," declared Mad Monk, "I haven't taught young women to paint like Mad Monk. Or like anyone else."

"I just use Mad Monk's name to get potential students interested in classes," continued Famous Art Teacher, "His reputation attracts artsy society types. My students already know of his 1000 Attitudes of Dalma portraits. His paintings are a great selling point. Of course none of my students will ever learn to paint like him. Only he can paint like him. But students need goals. Some even have dreams of fame and fortune. They don't want to be rich daughters, wives and mistresses forever. They want to be recognized as artists. I teach them to reach their goals. Or at least start on the way."

"I still want to know what you meant by 'if you know what I mean,'" repeated Mad Monk.

"You're a monk so you don't know the ways of the world. Put it like this. When young women are in a class with a great teacher they admire, they form attachments. They see this attachment as a way to transcend the rest of the students. They want to spend more time with their teacher. Sometimes that time gets intimate. Who can resist young women who throw themselves at you?"

"Ahhh, now I'm enlightened," said Mad Monk, "you say you teach young women how to paint like Mad Monk. You don't. You take money from their fathers, husbands and lovers. Then you seduce them. Then you have to leave town to find another new group of students."

"That sir monk is a brutal, blatant lie. The students throw themselves at me begging to be seduced. If I don't sleep with them they will leave my classes. What can I do? I have to make a living."

"What kind of life is that? Where's your sense of morality, of ethics, of meaning and purpose?"

"I had those once," said Famous Art Teacher wistfully, "I was a leader of student protests in the capitol. We wanted change. We wanted to stop wars. We wanted free health care for the poor and elderly. We wanted to stop the Emperor from taking everything from us and giving nothing back. Except to those men who did his work collecting taxes and leading the charge for war.

"In those days I painted bucolic pastoral landscapes with happy working people and sold them to wealthy collectors," Famous Art Teacher went on, "Some said my paintings reminded them of what our country could be if artists controlled everything. I had to hold my tongue or I'd be arrested and flogged.

"One day the inevitable crackdowns and repression arrived. So I did what all self-respecting artistic protestors do. I left the Capitol in a hurry with nothing but my skills and a few brushes, ink sticks and a roll of paper. What I didn't know is how many landscape artists were roaming the countryside trying to sell their work.

"Then one day I overheard two wealthy men discussing how they couldn't find a Mad Monk painting for a good price. Then it hit me. Make Mad Monk copies. I tried but failed miserably. I sold them in the market for almost nothing. They were just ordinary lifeless portraits that anyone with an uninspired hand could do. Then one day a wealthy collector approached me. He asked, 'Could you teach my daughter portrait painting?' Why not, I said. So we made a deal. From there it was just a few steps to classes, to the bedroom then escaping with my life."

"Interesting, interesting," mused Mad Monk. "I'd like to take your class. Do you have room?"

"Sure there's room in the arts for everyone. I don't care who you are as long as you have money. Classes start tomorrow afternoon in the village Assembly Hall."

Next day Mad Monk went back to the village. He entered the room where three beautifully dressed young women were sitting at tables learning to mix ink on stones, hold brushes and apply it to rice paper.

"Ah sir monk I'm glad you're here. Take this ink brush set, some paper sheets then get a cup of water. Try to imagine you're Mad Monk painting one of his masterpieces. Then paint what you see him doing. I'll come by in a few minutes to help you on your way to creating real art."

Mad Monk sat down alone at a small table in a corner of the room, mixed some ink and water, then painted a small portrait of Dalma. When he was finished he watched Famous Art Teacher instructing the giggling young women. "He certainly knows how to talk the art talk," mused Mad Monk.

Finally Famous Art Teacher came to Mad Monk's table. When he looked at Mad Monk's painting he said, "Come on sir monk stop fooling me. You brought this from the monastery. No one could paint like this in a few minutes except Mad Monk himself. Now paint one of your own. I'll be back in a few minutes."

With that Mad Monk picked up a brush, dipped it in the ink and again applied it to a sheet of rice paper. Just for fun he painted a small portrait of Dalma contemplating 'Teachers Are Made Not Born.'

When Famous Art Teacher returned to Mad Monk's table he looked at Mad Monk's new painting for a long minute, looked at Mad Monk with shock then bent down on his knees, bowed and exclaimed, "Painting Master 'Sunim' thank you for gracing our humble attempts at making art. I will now tell everyone that you approve my classes. That will help widen my reputation as a teacher."

With that Mad Monk tapped his forehead then ran back to his studio to paint Dalma contemplating 'Blind Ego Teaching Art.'

FEEDING TIGERS

One summer Mad Monk went seeking shamans, magicians and medicine men in hidden villages. He was on a long walking journey into the high mountain peaks. This was where sacred herbs, powerful medicinal mushrooms and mysterious magical roots are collected. He met many villagers who said they knew shamans but none were living nearby. He would have to go further on the way. He didn't mind wandering as long as there was a well stocked inn to rest in overnight.

One moonless star filled night on a flat mountaintop ridge they called Paik San-Shin 'White Magic Mountain' Mad Monk was taken by a guide to watch The Village Protector. Blazing torches cast long flickering theatrical light and shadows in a meadow otherwise surrounded by night's black blanket.

The absolute quiet became a dome of heavenly spirituality with a sense of deep mystical tension. In the darkness Mad Monk saw glowing dots of flame reflected eyes moving low, peering from above the carpet of animal grazed grasses. Silently an enormous white tiger moved cautiously, slowly, into view. In the firelight his beauty and power glowed like a statue in a shrine. He moved warily toward the kneeling blue robed old man holding meat scraps on a thin stick like a street vendor's kebab. The sounds of flickering flames were background music to a dangerous cat's feeding.

Mad Monk watched the eyes of man and beast momentarily transfixed into each other. The tiger carefully smelled the stick. Gingerly his mouth pulled the meat off then he ran back into the darkness.

Suddenly his guide grabbed Mad Monk by the wrist. He dragged a surprised Mad Monk to the center of the circle of light in front of the meat bucket. The villager picked up a long thin stick then dipped his free hand into the raw meat bucket, affixing his fist sized prize onto the stick's pointed end. He handed it to Mad Monk whispering, "This is real mountain life. Move away from the bucket. Kneel. Be silent. Don't show fear. Hold the meat high so the tiger can take it without taking your hand. The Forces of Nature and your power spirit will protect you."

Mad Monk quickly and quietly knelt holding out the stick mimicking the old man, the Village Protector, the Night Feeder.

Within minutes Mad Monk was looking into the fire lighted eyes of a thousand pound eternally hungry beast. Magnificent head held up high, it warily sniffed the air. It came toward Mad Monk, sniffed the meat, grabbed the morsel off the stick then ran back to its waiting pack.

Ordeal by voracious wild animal over, Mad Monk moved back from the center and smiled nervously to nodding, approving villagers. The feeding ritual continued until the bucket was empty. Hopefully all the tigers were well fed.

When Mad Monk returned to the village inn, his guide bought him a bottle of 'makoli' wine and spicy drinking snacks. "Thank you," said his guide, "now you too have prevented a man-eating rampage by hungry tigers. We think that's more important than finding shamans who live everywhere around here. They're as common as monks in a monastery. If they could really control Nature, they would stop tigers killing and eating our people. They can't.

"Our cure is simple. We feed the beasts butcher scraps. That's why we're not a vegan Buddhist village. We think it's better to eat meat then have butcher scraps left over. Much better than us being a tiger's meal."

When Mad Monk returned to his studio he painted Dalma contemplating 'The Good Butcher.'

"I still want to meet shamans," Mad Monk thought wistfully, "to understand why it's so difficult for them to control Nature if they have the ears of the Spirits."

WHO WHY HWADU

One beautiful day while walking on the way Mad Monk came upon an old monk playing a 'tungso' bamboo flute under a tree. He stopped to listen to the mesmerizing music. After some minutes the music stopped. The old monk musician opened his eyes, saw Mad Monk's puzzled look then explained, "I'm meditating on the most difficult 'hwadu' riddle of all time. Playing music helps me focus and concentrate. Whenever I stop playing it means I've come to a breakthrough. Almost. Problem is I can't remember the breakthrough after I've stopped."

"Who are you? Your music emanates blissful inner light and truth. I could listen all day," said Mad Monk appreciatively.

"I'm called Who Why."

"Are you contemplating Chao-shu's Dog?" asked Mad Monk.

"That's an easy one. Mu! Mu! Mu! and more Mu! It's for novices to make them feel like they're on the way to enlightenment once they understand the riddle in their own way. Mine is the supreme 'hwadu' riddle. Once I resolve it I will become a saint."

"Which one is it?"

"I call it 'Who Am I Really? Who am I not? Why? And why not?' It's the Inner Truth riddle. I was a respected teacher of 'hwadus.' I could talk for hours on what 'hwadus' do to create confusion and an open mind leading to enlightenment. Now my mind is frozen. I created this suffering for myself. I don't know what I'll do," replied Who Why.

"Hmmm. Yes. That's a difficult one. Many monks avoid it for fear of going insane. I've heard some monks become Naked Ascetics from the No-thing wrong turn of this 'hwadu.' They move to India where the Naked Ascetics go around naked after bathing in the sacred rivers. Good thing it's always warm and sunny there."

"So I've heard too. I can't do that because I get sunburn on my body and heatstroke in my head," replied Who Why.

"In my humble opinion it's not who you are or why you are that resolves this 'hwadu.' It's what you do. That's who and why you are. I walk, talk, paint and give charity. I'm happy with that so far. There are other things I do that are not so perfect. I'm very critical. I can offend people. Head Monk is always telling me I have an authority disrespect problem. He overlooks it most of the time because I contribute my earnings to the monastery.

"You make beautiful, mystical music but you suffer. Play for people not just for yourself. Make people go deep inside themselves with mystical melodies from your spirit. Then you will know who you are and why you are still alive. The answer to your 'hwadu' is Mindless Action. You're making yourself unhappy and sick with unnecessary meditation. Heaven gives us gifts but not for free. There are countless ways to pay for them. Find your way and know your own inner truth. Then you can change your name to 'Who Why What' as a reminder of what you do."

The old monk had tears in his eyes. He looked at Mad Monk then put his 'tungso' flute to his lips and began playing. Mad Monk listened until it was time to go walking on the way back to his studio.

When he arrived at his studio he painted Dalma contemplating, 'Music of the Seers.'

IMPULSIVE HERMIT

Mad Monk went walking on an out of the way trail to the dark side of the mountain. He came upon a man hopping around, slapping his thighs, waving his arms like a bird first on one foot then the other. When he stopped flailing he stared at a spot just off the trail. As he walked by Mad Monk asked, "Hello. Who are you? What are you doing?"

"My name is Impulsive Hermit. Let me ask your opinion," replied this out of breath man, "Should I build my hermitage above the road or below? Such difficult decisions."

"What's the difference?" asked Mad Monk.

"The difference? That's the most important part of selecting a location. I spend most of my time contemplating where to build my simple hut. This is my ninth in two years. Let's see if I build above I must carefully step down to get to the trail. Below I must climb up."

"I would imagine when you're carrying heavy things it's easier to go down," replied Mad Monk.

"Don't I have to carry them up first? This is more confusing than the last hermitage I built. I must get this hut building thing right this time. If not I will pitch a tent like the nomads use in summer."

"No respectable hermit lives in a tent. Maybe a yurt," said Mad Monk.

"You're right," said Impulsive Hermit, "My life is a constant hut building dilemma. I keep building huts that get destroyed by fires, mudslides, neighbors, animals, thieves, even other hut builders. My list of hut catastrophes goes on and on. Now I want to build just off this secluded trail. I've been contemplating a new hut here for a week. Will it last this time? I'm tired of moving."

"Go live in a monastery with other people like yourself," offered Mad Monk. The monks take care of everything. Food is pretty good. You don't have to carry it up a mountain. You can work in the garden with all the rest.

Water is clean from a well. And there are free self-defense classes. You can take some classes or meditate all you want. Or go hide in the forest. You can take actionless action and decide that no-thing is better than making a decision."

"I can't stand all the noise people make," retorted Impulsive Hermit, "I have very sensitive ears. And they all dress the same, no individuality. If one day I decide to wear red I don't want to be noticed or criticized. I loathe conformity from nonconformists. I'd rather take my chances alone in a hut than live with self-satisfied snobs. If they knew the true deepest inner truth they'd never think I'm different. I need to be alone or I end up criticizing people," said Impulsive Hermit as he started to hop about first one foot then the other.

"Why are you hopping around like that?" demanded Mad Monk.

"Coo coo roo! Coo coo roo! Chik chik chik! I can't help myself. I'm impulsive."

Mad Monk tapped his forehead then walked quickly back to his studio to paint Dalma contemplating people who are 'Never Satisfied.'

MASKED MONK

While walking on the way in the middle of the landscaped village park Mad Monk came upon a young monk reading aloud from a piece of paper. He stopped to listen for a few minutes. The monk was reading a new and unique 'iyagi', a parable with a moral ending.

When the young monk finished reading Mad Monk walked over to him. "Who are you? Your story is inspiring and enlightening. Why don't you read it at our monastery?"

"Oh I could never do that. My name is Shy Storyteller. I have terrible stage fright. I sweat and shake. I get tongue-tied. My mind tells me people don't like me and what I'm saying. I want to run off-stage and hide. I can only read outside where Nature is the audience. So here I am."

Mad Monk thought then said, "Maybe I can help you. I used to be like you. That's why I chose to paint the 1000 Attitudes of Dalma. I stand invisible behind my paintings. They exist without my presence. I don't have to be a performer to show my dedication. I learned to let go of worrying about what people think of me. It wasn't easy. Now they only think of my work."

"I wish I could paint like you," responded Shy Storyteller, "but I can't. My dedication is writing these 'iyagi' stories. I see the worlds of men, women and Nature interacting in many good and sometimes bad ways. I tried to teach in the monastery but couldn't. The students just laughed at me when I tried to read sutras aloud. I stuttered hopelessly. Never again."

"Let's go," said Mad Monk taking Shy Storyteller to his studio near the Temple. There he put a grey silk cloth bag over the shy writer monk's head. He cut out holes for nose, mouth and eyes.

That afternoon Mad Monk introduced "Masked Monk" at the monastery's Assembly Hall. Then Masked Monk read his stories with deep feeling, projection and confidence. Everyone listened with total attention. Afterward the awed and satisfied gathering nodded and applauded their approval.

"You see," proclaimed Mad Monk after Masked Monk's first reading, "You read your stories with power and emotion. No stuttering, no running away. Everyone loved them. Now you can take off that mask."

"Thank you Painting Master 'sunim' for showing me how to present myself without fear," replied Masked Monk, "Your teaching has inner truth. There's always a way to overcome obstacles. As for my mask, I will never take it off. I like being called Masked Monk. As you like being called Mad Monk. From now on I will write stories and read them in public wearing my mask. Do you think you could make another one in case something happens to this one?"

Mad Monk tapped his forehead. "I thought I was helping you gain confidence. Now I see I was helping you find a costume for a character. You must learn to make as many masks as you need. Just make sure you continue writing as yourself."

Then Mad Monk ran back to his studio to paint Dalma contemplating 'Masks We Wear To Be Who We Really Are.'

MICHIN IYAGI
(Crazy Storyteller)

While walking on the way near the stream's edge Mad Monk came upon a man kneeling on his knees staring into the stream's softly flowing water. Mad Monk walked over, quietly got down on his own knees then watched the man as he stared into the stream in deep meditation. Mad Monk thought for a moment to join him in this calming water reflection.

Suddenly a stone thrown by a boy from across the stream plopped into the water making endless ripples. The man looked at the ripples for a moment then emerged as from a dream. He turned and saw Mad Monk watching him.

"What were you looking at in the stream? You're dressed like a villager so logically you're not a fisherman. You are interesting to me. What's your name?" asked Mad Monk.

"I'm called 'Michin Iyagi' Crazy Storyteller. I was divining my future until that boy threw a rock at me. When water meditation works I go into a deep trance. Then I grasp the water's True Nature which is also my own.

I channel characters and stories. Water can only tell the truth. Then I use these truths to write parables.

"In this stream there are smooth and rough surfaces," continued Michin Iyagi, "on the ever changing bottom, big and small rocks shadow where fish hide like people scared or ashamed. The surface is smooth like a happy family. In sunlight its reflection glitters with flashes of enlightenment so brilliant I cannot stare for long. This is how my stories are made. Like the layers of a stream. Rocky bottoms are the body of my stories with its twists and turns as in character's lives. Ripples are flowing obstacles to be overcome. Fish breaking smooth surface water with a loud splash is the exciting climax. Quiet reflection leads to knowing the true inner self. Then there's all important laughter. Without laughter a parable is like a funeral. The moral must be ironic in the Chan/Zen way."

"That's very interesting," said Mad Monk, "I always thought stories were dialogues between a monk, teacher, sunim and students. I didn't know people made them up without a teacher to record."

"I hear and see stories," said Michin Iyagi, "when I meditate while staring into this stream. There are teachers and students rising from the bottom to the surface reflecting on their minds' true inner natures. Everything I ever wanted to know about the mind is reflected from this stream. I've tried to show it to others but this stream only speaks to me."

"I take long walks arm in arm with my imagination on our way to my painting studio," said Mad Monk. I see and hear Nature. I observe the intertwined worlds of humanity. There is always something inspiring. Endless flashes of life both high and low send me running to my studio. I couldn't live without my daily walks. Today I walked here and met you."

"What's your name? You sound like an interesting monk," asked Michin Iyagi.

"I'm called Mad Monk. I live and paint in the San Shin Temple monastery above the village."

"Ah of course," said Michin Iyagi happily, "we have met for a Heaven arranged reason. I don't know what it is yet but we shall find out. Everything is for a reason and everything comes with a story."

"Your story art is the literary brother of my work," declared Mad Monk, "I paint the 1000 Attitudes of Dalma. Each painting is inspired by our experiences channeled through ink and brush. I translate Dalma's contemplations on the world and Heaven as I believe he sees it. He speaks through me but not to me. He would scorn the way I live. I drink, sing

and carouse with villagers, fornicate with women and eat forbidden foods. It's the contradictory way of my life. I'm a monk and common man in the same mind. I believe Dalma forgives my indiscretions since he continues to let me paint his portraits."

"How did you become Dalma's painter?" asked Michin Iyagi.

"When I was a boy I loved drawing and painting. One day I walked to the Temple to see the paintings. After a test of my painting potential I was chosen by the monastery's old Painting Master 'Sunim' to become his novice. I started painting Dalma very young. I was innocent then. I continue serving him to this day. Even though I'm less innocent now."

"Do you know the small inn in the village next to yours?" asked Michin Iyagi, "I will be there tonight with some friends. I invite you to join us. They are writers, poets and artists. I think you will like them."

With that Michin Iyagi and Mad Monk stood up, bowed then walked away in opposite directions.

That night Mad Monk put on his commoner's suit then walked to the next village's inn. He easily found it by following the happy noises of men drinking and laughing. Inside sitting at a round table were Michin Iyagi with his friends. There was an empty cushion.

"We held this for you," explained Michin Iyagi. "I'm about to tell the story of how I became an 'iyagi' story writer and teller.

"My story starts when Heavenly Dalma was walking on his mission to the East. He walked through my monastery after a sutra preaching. For some reason I still can't explain I followed him to the stream that was on the way.

"Suddenly he sat down. I thought he would take a drink and meditate there. It's a very clear clean stream.

"Even though I was scared I worked up the courage to sit beside him. After a while I sensed he could feel my presence so I asked him the most important question I ever asked anyone, "Great Enlightened Master and Enlightening Teacher of Teachers I'm a young man who can't get stories out of my mind no matter how long or intensely I meditate. The masters at this monastery suggest that I try harder to achieve enlightenment and understand no-thing like the other young monks. Then I too could become a dedicated monk. However stories stop me from being like everyone else.

"I love my stories like a father loves his children," I rambled crazily yet still sensing that Dalma was listening to me, "I want the masters to like me. Can you in your infinite wisdom guide me?"

"Dalma sat staring at me with his big round dark eyes. He said nothing. Then he pointed to the stream. I looked towards the water. It was clear and placid as it has always been, "Master I don't understand.""

"He stood up, grabbed me by the ear so I had to stand, pulled me to the stream's edge then screamed in my ear, "Look! All stories are in there!" Then he threw me into the stream. At that moment as I broke the water's surface I was enlightened.

"As I sat on the shallow bottom looking at Dalma from the surface I saw his reflection in the water as he floated away to the East. From that day to this I meditate at that stream. Water has taught me there's always another story."

When Michin Iyagi's story ended everyone smiled and applauded then filled each other's cups with 'makoli' wine. They drank to Michin Iyagi the Crazy Storyteller and of course each other's health. After a few more drinks and toasts to art, philosophy and love Mad Monk grabbed his lantern and went back to his studio where he painted Dalma contemplating the 'Mysterious Ways of Inspiration.'

He knew he'd return to that inn one day soon.

POOR HERB FARMER

Mad Monk was walking on the way near the edge of the forest where it meets the productive small farms. He had just sold a big Dalma painting to a rich collector. He was on his way to the monastery to give them the proceeds minus his own small amount for what he called his 'Mad Monk Money'.

He was proud of the farmers. He was friendly with a few. He thought if he hadn't been a painter he would be a farmer. As he looked around he saw a young farmer sitting in the middle of a verdant herb garden loudly moaning "I am here because they are coming. I can't go home. No one will help me."

Mad Monk walked over to him. "Why are you sitting there? Who are they? What's your name?"

"I'm called Poor Herb Farmer. I'm waiting for the animals, insects and birds that eat my herb crops. I know they will return. They always do. I must be here to stop them. Since I don't eat animal flesh, I figure they owe me money. If they're going to eat my crops, then they must pay.

"I'm sitting here to protect my herbs. Which I am told by everyone are the most flavorful. That's because I mix a secret compost fertilizer. The recipe was whispered down for generations in my family. The other farmers are envious of my crops. Unfortunately I must sit here all night saving them from ravenous creatures. There must be a better way. I love farming but this is too much. I miss my family." he said sadly.

"Have you been home lately?" asked Mad Monk.

"No. I have three little children. But I must save my herbs or we all will go hungry."

After a moment's reflection Mad Monk offered, "I will sit here tonight so you can go home. Kindly return with a little food and drink if you have extra."

"Oh could you kind and generous monk," said Poor Herb Farmer. "Be sure to stay wide awake tonight. That's when the animals come out to eat. Dalma bless us for your compassion."

"Go now," said Mad Monk, "your crops are in good hands." Then Poor Herb Farmer left for home.

As night spread its dark blanket Mad Monk began to feel cold. Luckily he had a gourd flask of 'makoli' wine in his bag. He drank it all then fell deeply asleep. Naturally rabbits, moles, chipmunks, deer and birds stopped by the herb garden to feast. They just ignored the soundly snoring monk.

At dawn next morning Poor Herb Farmer returned to find Mad Monk fast asleep. He kicked Mad Monk who awoke with a fright. Poor Herb Farmer screamed at him, "What have you done! My beautiful garden is gone! My family will starve. I am ruined. You are not a good monk." The farmer began to weep.

"My friend," countered Mad Monk, "no need to worry. Everything is good. I collected money from each and every animal that ate here. I have it right here for you." From his shoulder bag Mad Monk took out the bag of coins gained from his recent painting sale. He showed it to Poor Herb Farmer, "Sorry to report, I couldn't get a cent from the slugs so I told the birds to eat them. Which they happily did."

"Can this be true, oh holy one?" asked the farmer grabbing the bag. "Nature is a universal restaurant," declared Mad Monk, "everything living is always hungry. Some live. Some die. Some pay. Some don't."

"What's your name?" asked Poor Herb Farmer.

"Mad Monk."

"Please sir tell me the secret of collecting money from the animals."

"It's easy when you learn to talk nicely to them in their own languages," replied Mad Monk.

"How can you? Please teach me, 'sunim.'"

"Did I say I could talk to animals? My mistake. It's so early. I meant I could talk to farmers. Ask the other farmers how they keep the animals and birds away from their crops. They might reveal their techniques if you share your secret fertilizer formula."

With that Mad Monk tapped his forehead then ran away back to his studio where he painted Dalma contemplating 'Humanity Shares Nature's Restaurant.'

RITUAL SACRIFICES

Mad Monk went on a hiking pilgrimage of southern Korean Buddhist shrines. He wore his commoner suit because the road was very dry and dusty. He painted each shrine on sheets of Hanji paper. When he ran out of art supplies he went into a village to buy paper and ink. In this particular village on this particular day he walked by a 'mudang' shaman with a band of traditional musicians. On low tables around the shaman 'kut' ritual stage were arrayed fresh fruit and sweet pastry offerings. The 'mudang's' was dancing, chanting and performing a 'kut' shamanic ritual.

"What's this 'kut' for?" asked Mad Monk.

"To attract rich people to this new gallery," replied one of the 'mudang's' helpers.

"I thought a gallery needs good art, not the Heavenly spirits' help."

"Sometimes it needs both," the 'mudang's' helper pointed out. "All we need to complete the ritual is the dog sacrifice. I'll be right back."

"No! You mustn't sacrifice a dog or any animal," insisted Mad Monk. "Only human sacrifice can properly beg spirits' help. I'll be back within a few minutes with the perfect sacrifice."

Mad Monk tapped his forehead then ran to the art supply shop. He bought what he needed including a needle for sewing scrolls. Then right there in the shop he began painting. In a few minutes he was done. He mounted the 'hanji' mulberry paper painting on a hemp scroll, rolled it up then ran back to the ritual 'mudang' kut.

The helper was holding down a whimpering dog for the sacrifice. The 'mudang' held a knife to its throat.

"Stop!" screamed Mad Monk, "Here's a human sacrifice."

He handed the scroll to the 'mudang' who said, "What kind of trick is this? We must finish this 'kut' to get paid."

"Is the gallery owner here?" asked Mad Monk.

"Yes I'm here," answered a voice in the crowd.

"Come forward. Unroll the scroll," directed Mad Monk. On it was an image of Dalma sitting in a ring of fire. "Now use this sewing needle to draw a few drops of your blood. Be sure to drop some on Dalma's image. This is a real human blood sacrifice. This is also my sacrifice for the life of that dog. Sell this picture so everyone gets paid a little more without an animal sacrifice. I will take this dog away from here. Let him die as a proud animal. As any of you would like. None of us wants to be sacrificed. Now this painting comes with a story. Tell it. It makes the painting worth much more. Gallery owner I wish you all the business you deserve."

With that Mad Monk took the dog on the rope, went back to the art supply shop, picked up his things then continued on his pilgrimage.

The 'mudang' and gallerist looked at each other in surprised wonder. "Who was that man?" asked the 'mudang'.

"I don't know. I must find out," replied the gallerist, "Although I think he's mad, he paints a great Dalma. Perhaps he was once a monk. I should represent him."

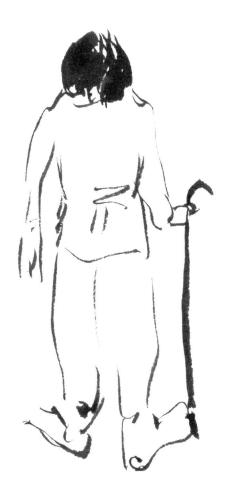

SIZE DOES MATTER

Mad Monk brought a painting to a new collector's large, opulent home. He unrolled the scroll for him.

"Why is this painting so small?" asked the collector.

"Let go of comparing," replied Mad Monk, "then you will see it's exactly the right size for what it is."

"It will get lost on my big walls. Paintings have to be big to get noticed here."

"Then it will be found by those taking the time to seek enlightenment," Mad Monk answered.

"There's truth to that. I will buy it only if you paint me a bigger one specially for my big walls."

"Now that I know what you want, it can be done," said Mad Monk smiling.

With that Mad Monk tapped his forehead, left the rich new collector's home, ran back to his studio. There he painted a very large expensive portrait of Dalma contemplating 'Big is the Way to a Rich Man's Heart.'

ARMED SHROOMDOG

Wearing his street clothes Mad Monk sat in the village inn drinking and telling stories with his friends. He always felt he was less intimidating in street clothes. He could be Mad Monk without looking like a monk.

A man came in carrying a basket of mushrooms. He walked over to the grill then asked the cook, "Kindly grill these. I want them tasty and delicious for the man who hunted them all day. Me." He put some coins on the grillman's counter.

Now Mad Monk loved grilled mushrooms more than anything else.

He went over to the mushroom hunter and asked if he could buy one from him. The man refused his offer, "To truly appreciate these mushrooms you have to search for them in the forest. These are better than any grown on farms. Find your own mushrooms. They will taste better. These are mine."

Mad Monk was disappointed. He knew he wasn't supposed to be attached to desires but for mushrooms he made an exception. Now he had a yearning insatiable taste for grilled mushrooms. Since he was a little drunk he began to talk. "The reason I don't search for wild mushrooms anymore is the terrible Giant Slug who lives in a forest cave. The first time I saw him I knew I'd never go there again.

"He's very quiet, slowly slithering along the forest floor eating all the mushrooms in his path. He also leaves a trail of blood and tears from the unsuspecting villagers he's eaten.

"If you bend over to cut a mushroom," Mad Monk continued, "he silently sneaks up behind you, jumps on your neck, then sucks you dry from the outside in. Blood, guts and slime. You are a very brave man to go into that forest alone." Then Mad Monk walked away shaking his head, holding in his laughter until he was outside.

A few days later Mad Monk was walking in the forest wearing his monk suit. He came upon the same grilled mushroom eater carrying a spear with a sharp metal tip under his arm. He had a high power bow with a quiver of arrows pulled onto his shoulders. Long knives and a hatchet rested in the warrior belt around his waist. In his free hand he carried a large wicker basket full of beautiful fresh picked forest mushrooms.

"Hello Mr. Mushroom Hunter. What's your name and why are you so heavily armed?" asked Mad Monk, "Is there a war happening in this forest? If there is I must avoid it. I don't think I'm meant to die today."

The hunter laughed. Then said, "Don't worry there's no war right now. My name is Armed Shroomdog. I'm out here foraging for my dinner. What's your name sir monk?"

"I'm Mad Monk. Why are you armed with so many weapons?"

"Haven't you heard? There's a ferocious man eating Giant Slug that eats mushrooms by the barrel full. It can swallow mushroom hunters whole. It's living in this forest. Everyone's afraid of it. However I love eating wild mushrooms so much I'm willing to take my chances meeting him. If I do I'm ready for all out battle. He won't suck the life out of me."

"Ah yes I've heard of the Giant Slug," said Mad Monk, "in fact I met a monk who knew a man who forced the Giant Slug to leave the forest on the other side of this mountain. He told me that the Giant Slug said he would stop eating mushroom hunting villagers if they would sacrifice a virgin to him.

"Fortunately for the villagers, but unfortunately for her, they found an unattractive teenage orphan girl living in the countryside, tied her up and put her in front of the Giant Slug's cave. When they returned in a few days they were both gone. Vanished. It was safe to be back in that forest on the other side of the mountain."

Armed Shroomdog said, "So that's why the Giant Slug moved here. Is he living in the caves at the base of this mountain now?"

"I believe that's where he would go," replied Mad Monk, "because he needs wet dark places to live. I don't know if this village can find any virgins they can sacrifice. Come to think of it I'm a monk and represent the precepts of virtuous service. I'm sure slugs know monks are virgins. I will go sit in front of the caves by the base of the mountain. I will sacrifice myself for the villagers. That is the highest dedication of charity. Your part is you must put your basket of mushrooms out there with me to attract the Giant Slug."

"You would do that for us?" Armed Shroomdog asked seriously.

There was a long silent pause. "No," replied Mad Monk, "Just kidding."

Armed Shroomdog pointed his spear at Mad Monk's heart. "You will go sit at the cave's entrance or I'll bring your dead body there. I will hunt mushrooms without fear of monsters eating me."

"Before you do that," said Mad Monk, "you should know I made up the Giant Slug story when I was drunk at the inn. I wasn't wearing my monk's suit.

The story is about letting go of your fears. You believed it even though it's a tall tale. Now I see that your way of letting go of fear is to arm yourself and kill whatever makes you afraid. That is no way to live in peace and harmony."

"What is your name again?"

"Mad Monk."

"Ahhh! Of course. Mad Monk. You say outrageous things. They say you paint brilliant pictures showing many Attitudes of Dalma. I've never seen one however I hear they are inspiring. That's why I won't kill you today."

When Mad Monk realized he had come very close to death he tapped his forehead. "Thank you for enlightening me about telling stories that can make men kill. I will know better from now on." Then he turned and slowly walked away with his head down.

He returned to his studio that night to paint Dalma contemplating 'Tall Tales that Kill the Teller.'

Mad Monk swore to himself he would never tell the story of the Giant Slug again, "Even though I'm sure it really exists somewhere in my mind's dark wet forest where I'm surrounded by many healthy edible mushrooms ready for picking."

SUPERIOR STATUS

Mad Monk was invited to the opening of a newly built yet traditionally styled inn a few villages away from his monastery. It was a beautiful day. It had rained the previous night. The roads were muddy so he decided to walk there wearing his commoner clothes that weren't of the newest fashion or highest quality. After all he was a monk. "This is me," he thought, "take me as I really am. Rumpled truths expose well dressed lies."

By the time he reached the new inn's celebration there were dozens of people sitting at outdoor tables drinking 'soju' wine from small cups and eating 'ban chan' finger foods. He was surprised how well dressed everyone was. Not like in his village inn where workers gathered at the end of the day.

Mad Monk went inside the traditional yet modern building. Everything appeared to be made of the highest quality. "Obviously the most skilled craftsmen worked here," he thought, "I wonder who owns this inn? He or she must be wealthy with good taste. Perhaps I could sell a painting."

A woman in traditional costume came toward him carrying a tray of small handmade ceramic cups full of Andong 'soju', the best and most expensive traditional Korean wine. He took one, shouted "Kumpai!" so loudly that all noise in the room stopped. Everyone had to look. Mad Monk swallowed it down on one gulp. "These are very small cups," thought Mad Monk. He went looking for the waitress to get another.

A woman wearing an elegant traditional 'hanbok' dress like a silk weaver's masterpiece of design and color hurriedly walked up to him. "Excuse me," she condescendingly asked, "are you an invited guest? This is a private opening for my new inn. For friends only."

Realizing he wasn't wearing his clean monk's suit he said, "I'm from a village a few miles away. The one near the monastery. I was walking on my way home when I saw this crowd. I simply wandered in. You have created a very beautiful inn. I hope you have success and happiness. What is your name?"

"Thank you," she said. " I'm called 'Superior Status.' Coincidentally, I know Mad Monk the famous painter who lives in the monastery in your village. He's a very good friend of mine. He promised to give me one of his masterpieces for my walls. I expect him here any minute. You do know him of course? He's very important."

Mad Monk's impish mind suddenly flipped into full thrust. "No I don't. But I've heard he's really quite mad. Not someone to trust. He's always playing tricks on people and saying outrageous things. I keep far away from men like that."

"Yes he's mad. He gets away with it because he's a brilliant painter. I can think of many times when I was with him he acted the perfect gentleman. Then without cause he would say something very lewd and suggestive. Like a common drunken peasant. Not like a monk who has taken vows not to desire women or indulge in sexual misconduct.

"Just between us, I once had to fight him off when he got very drunk. He told me 'you're the most beautiful woman in the world. I have to make love to you here and now.' What could I do? He's such a smooth talker and so strong. I let him have his way. You can imagine the rest. That's why he's called the Mad Monk. But I still love and respect him."

Mad Monk stared at her and thought, "I've never met this woman before. She's asking me if I know me. Then she tells me a story about me. What does she want?"

"I'm glad I don't know him," replied Mad Monk, "he sounds like a bad influence on good people. Thank you for this drink. I have to go now." He tapped his forehead, bowed politely and left.

He ran back to his studio. When he reached it he put on his monk's suit. Then he sat down to paint Dalma contemplating 'Well Dressed Status Games.'

When he was done he rolled it up then returned to the new inn's opening. When he arrived even more people were drinking free wine. The room was loud with laughter.

Mad Monk found Superior Status. She was so drunk she didn't recognize him dressed as a monk. She saw him, sauntered up to him and asked, "Who are you, kind monk? This is a party for drinkers. Do you drink? If so you are welcome."

"I'm Mad Monk. If I remember correctly we know each other very well. I brought you this painting I promised you when I seduced you. Here it is." He jumped up onto a table then unrolled the scroll. Turning around he showed it to the drunken guests.

Suddenly he yelled over the crowd, "This is my gift for our hostess. She has a good story about why I brought this. When she finishes that one ask her to tell you the truth."

With that he jumped down, handed the scroll to Superior Status demanding, "Put this up on your wall. Look at it and remember me. You'll pay for the painting with free drinks for me whenever I come for you."

With that he tapped his forehead, grabbed another cup of 'soju' wine and ran away.

USUAL POLITICS

Mad Monk was walking along the way into the village. In the central square he came upon a well dressed man giving out handbills with this headline:

EVERYTHING IS HORRIBLE IN ITS OWN WAY!
I'M THE ONLY ONE WHO CAN FIX EVERYTHING!
VOTE FOR ME BEFORE IT'S TOO LATE!

"This is very interesting to me," said Mad Monk to this man, "How is it possible you can fix everything when no one can possible know everything since everything is ever changing into different everything. And what is horrible for one person may be sublime paradise for another. What's your name?"

"I'm called Usual Politics. Pleased to meet you. However, as I'm sure you know very well you are a naïve monk living in a sheltered world away from people and their problems. You know nothing of how the real world works. There are great injustices and terrible heart breaking disasters everywhere. I can fix it. I can make the world beautiful again. Who are you good monk?"

"I'm called Mad Monk. I have different eyes than you. I've walked everywhere. I've seen great and small sights and done almost everything on my walks. To me the world isn't horrible. I do something new and beautiful every day. You should travel more. It broadens your mind and deepens compassion in your heart. Please excuse my pride. I'm not supposed to brag."

"Yes I agree. I love to travel. However I'm a politician. I do what I do and say what I say to get elected. It's my role in society. After I'm elected I will use tax money to travel the world in first class."

"But you're not telling the truth," opined Mad Monk, "tell people the truth. You must let go of lying. Lies fool the people who believe in you. Lies destroy you. Your soul will suffer sooner or later."

"Perhaps, perhaps not," said Usual Politics, "Truth is relative. To some people, hopefully a majority, I'm telling the truth. They're the ones who will elect me."

"Ah, of course. I understand now," said Mad Monk, "Politicians are like dedicated monks: true believers in enlightenment and transcendence who keep our monastery and its teachings alive. You are teaching the people fear and paranoia so you get elected. You are keeping the Political System alive. Dedication gives life meaning. Thank you for this worldly enlightenment."

"You're very welcome, Mad Monk," said Usual Politics, "Now that we know each other like brothers can you help get monks to vote for me?"

With that Mad Monk tapped his forehead and ran away to his studio where he painted Dalma contemplating 'Political Lies and False Promises.'

TOO MUCH EVERYTHING

One of Mad Monk's richest collectors named Too Much Everything invited Mad Monk for a cruise on what he bragged was the 'biggest yacht on the water.' The big boat was docked on Peace Lake, which was shared by local fishermen and rich pleasure boat sailors alike.

Mad Monk thought he would meet some of Too Much Everything's friends, perhaps sell some paintings to benefit the Monastery. "A painter does what he must to keep monks fed," Mad Monk mused, "even spend a day eating, drinking and fishing with rich businessmen."

As they set sail Mad Monk talked to Too Much Everything, "I've seen brilliant paintings of this lake surrounded by those high peaks in heavy clouds. What made those paintings come alive were the tiny fishermen working in their small boats. It's a meditation on the coexistence of Man and Nature."

"Who cares about them?" replied Too Much Everything curtly, "I don't. I can buy fresh fish any time I want. Every day these damned fishermen beg me to buy from them."

"Why don't you?" asked Mad Monk. "They're just trying to make a living. They have families."

"Because they are pests. If I show them any attention they'll never leave me alone to enjoy a day in peace and quiet on this glorious lake. We have to get control over them."

Mad Monk looked around at the dozen or so people who were enjoying the good life on Too Much Everything's yacht. He wondered if they all loathed fishermen.

They set sail heading out to the middle of the enormous lake. They dropped anchor in a spot with no other boats near by. Then the Captain and crew brought out expensive wines and gourmet foods for the guests. As they were dining a small fishing boat came to the yacht's side. Suddenly there was a yell from below, "Very good fresh fish today. From the deep water. Rich man can eat the best fish. Good price. Very good price."

"We don't want any," yelled Too Much Everything as he leaned over the yacht's side rail, "Go away. You're annoying us. We're here for a day of pleasure cruising not haggling over fish prices."

Again shouts were heard, "Good price for rich man. I have fresh fish today from this lake. Very good price. Bring home to beautiful rich wife. She love you a lot."

Too Much Everything yelled back at the fisherman, "Move away from my boat or I'll order my crew to sail over your pathetic puny little boat. That will teach you a lesson."

"Too Much Everything is very arrogant," thought Mad Monk, "he doesn't understand fishermen's lives. He only wants to impress his business friends with how tough he can be. He is also cruel to threaten people struggling to live. I wish I hadn't come on his boat today. Collectors should be seen only to relieve them of their money. Never a good idea to socialize with them."

The fisherman sensed he wouldn't make any sales that day then shrugged and slowly rowed away.

As the yacht was heading back to shore a fierce storm blew down from the mountains. Wildly screaming wind gusts knocked the yacht around at will. There wasn't time to bring down the sails. The boat was rocking in every direction. Rain was pounding down on everything and everyone. Thunder roared. Lightning crackled. Then the loudest longest thunderbolt Mad Monk had ever heard hit the yacht's mast, cracking it in half. The top of the mast fell onto the boat. Luckily no one was hurt.

Just as suddenly the storm passed on, raging over wildly confused water into mountains on the opposite shore. The sky was again clear and blue. Mad Monk like everyone on deck wondered how we would get back to shore. The Captain said, "We will have to man the lifeboats and row back."

"Row like those fisherman? Never!" yelled Too Much Everything. Captain, fix this mast. What am I paying you for?"

"I'm not a ship's carpenter. I'm a captain. I sail," he countered.

Everyone stood watching as Too Much Everything lost his temper. "Do something or you're fired. I'd like to throw you overboard."

"Don't blame me. I didn't bring the storm," replied the captain. "Blame the Heavens if you must blame."

While they argued a small fishing boat sidled up to the damaged yacht. A voice from below yelled, "Do you need help? I can try to tow you into shore. It will be slow but all boats float on the same water."

The captain looked over the side and saw the fisherman who Too Much Everything had chased away. "I can throw you a tow line from the bow. Catch it and see if you can tow us in."

Too Much Everything looked over the side. He asked, "Why would you help us after I chased you away?"

"Because you're lucky everyone isn't like you. I still have fresh fish at a very good price. I will tow you into shore even if you don't buy from me."

When they arrived at the shore Too Much Everything's guests bought all the fisherman's catch of the day.

Mad Monk went back to his studio to paint Dalma contemplating 'Arrogance Needs Generosity to Survive.'

TRASH THE RICH

One cloudy night Mad Monk was walking back from the village inn with an empty sack over his shoulder. He had a good night distributing food to the poor and of course to his old mother. Along the way he came upon a man dumping trash on the side of the beautiful path leading to the monastery and Temple complex.

"Excuse me friend," asked Mad Monk firmly, "Why are you leaving your trash here instead of at the village recycling center? What's your name?"

"My name is Trash the Rich. I leave my trash here to show these elite hypocrite bastards who travel this road not everyone is as content with society and government as they. It's my political statement against The Repulsive Powers That Be."

"Dumping your trash here only means I will pick it up as a public service then bring it to the recycling center. Your enemies will never know how you feel."

"Ahhh. That explains why nothing ever changes in this village, province or country. You can't do this to me. You're stopping progress. You're one of the oppressors."

"I'm not your enemy. I only want a naturally beautiful, clean path to my studio, monastery and Temple. If that's elitist then call me the Emperor's Brother. Besides there are other ways to show your discontent."

"What can the little man do? Trash is what I have."

"Write poems, stories and songs. Stand up in the village square. People will like you. They will gather. They will listen. Just like we monks gather at the Temple."

"Others have tried that. They were arrested and executed."

"I didn't say preaching insurrection isn't without risks. But if it's what you really want then accept the risks and be happy knowing you're in the advance guard of progress. You never know. You may succeed. However if you throw trash here again I will have you arrested for littering."

"You see, I'm right. I know you're one of the rich bastards. All you care about is beauty. People are starving. People are sick and dying. Can't you see that too?"

"Come with me," asked Mad Monk, "to feed the poor and comfort the lonely as we monks do. You will make the world a better and cleaner place."

"Then I will take their trash to throw in the eyes of the oppressors."

Mad Monk looked at Trash the Rich for a moment. Then he tapped himself on his forehead. "I too am a believer in progress. That's why I feed the poor. I believe the Emperor will one day supply food from his warehouses for everyone, not just his Royal Court and soldiers. Until then I do what I can. I too am making a revolution. A peaceful caring one. Never would I throw dirty trash along the way. We don't need revolution if there isn't natural beauty."

Mad Monk then picked up Trash the Rich's droppings and walked away smiling. Trash the Rich walked the opposite way. He was never seen again on Mad Monk's path.

Mad Monk returned to his studio where he painted Dalma contemplating 'Cleaning Up Also Changes The World.'

TRUTHFUL GAMBLER

Walking on the way past the 'tai kwan do' martial arts practice field Mad Monk came upon a novice monk punching his fist into a bucket of sand. Not uncommon as that's one of the practices for a fighter's training. However this monk was screaming, "Wife! Mother-in-law! Sister-in-law! Brothers-in-law! Father-in-law! Neighbors! Forgive me!" punch after punch repeating the same mantra.

Mad Monk watched him for a minute then walked up to him. "Who are you? What are you screaming about?"

"I am called Truthful Gambler. I'm here repenting for my betrayals to my wife's family and friends. I ruined them because of my gambling problem. This monastery is the last resort for me. Next time I get into gambling debt I will commit suicide."

Truthful Gambler was wearing the saddest, most ashamed and self deprecating face Mad Monk had ever seen. "How did this happen?"

"I was a life long gambler until I came here. Sometimes I won big. However usually I lost more than I won. I was in debt. I stole my wife's family heirlooms then sold them to pay off my debts. I blamed a poor neighbor who didn't have an alibi. He was beaten by the sheriff until he couldn't work so his family had to sell themselves into servitude. When I saw that I wept to myself in shame. I told my good wife I had to leave the family to follow the religious life. I told her I was inspired by the words of Dalma. I didn't tell her about my gambling, my stealing or my false testimony. Worst part is I still owe money to the gang. If they find me and I don't pay up they will kill me." Then he punched into the sand bucket repeating the same pathetic pleading confession.

For a few minutes Mad Monk stepped away but still watched Truthful Gambler. He thought about the myriad obstacles to enlightenment that life throws at all humans even the most pure. He thought of himself and his own hedonist vices. He felt very lucky he wasn't also a gambler. His thrill, he realized, came from walking on the way and painting the 1000 Attitudes of Dalma. And of course a few forbidden pleasures.

Mad Monk walked back to Truthful Gambler. "Perhaps I can help save your life. I'm called Mad Monk. I paint portraits of Dalma that sell for very high prices to collectors. I will give you a picture to take to the city art market. You can sell it to pay off your debts and return the lost property to your family. Then you must leave this monastery. I don't think you are here to seek enlightenment. You will only cause yourself misery from lack of dedication. You can't punch sand all day. If you stay, you must also work in the vegetable fields, help maintain our buildings, study and obey our rules. Come to my studio tonight. I will give you a picture. Tell no one."

"Thank you Mad Monk," Truthful Gambler said bowing, "you have saved my life and restored me to my family. I will be there tonight."

Mad Monk went back to his studio and painted Dalma contemplating 'Real Tragedies' using the sad face of Truthful Gambler for inspiration.

That night Truthful Gambler arrived and received a scroll. "I don't want to see you here again," admonished Mad Monk, "Give up gambling forever. Find a suitable way to get money for your family. Be a strong member of your community."

Several months later Mad Monk had a well dressed visitor. "Do you remember me? I'm Truthful Gambler."

"What are you doing here? I told you never to come back."

"Hear me out. After I gave your painting to the gallery, the owner told me I get 50 percent of the sale price. He gets 50 percent commission. I said "What for?"

"Because I know the people who want to collect and invest in art."

"It was enough to pay my debts and buy back my family's property," Truthful Gambler continued, "I was restored. I stayed around art market a few days waiting for the picture to sell. I watched and easily figured out how it works. It's all about dressing well and having a story to tell. After I paid off my debts I did the right thing by my family. I kept some of the money, bought this suit and I'm opening a gallery. I'd like you to be one of my artists. I believe I can sell your paintings to rich gangsters for a much better price. I'll tell them it's an investment."

Mad Monk tapped his forehead. "Ahh yes. That would mean more money for the monastery. We'll try it. I will give you one picture at a time. I hope selling art is as great a thrill as gambling."

"Once they hear I'm working with you many artists will seek me out. I'm a respectable member of the community now."

"Then we will change your name to Art Gambler. More appropriate for a gallery owner."

Mad Monk gave Art Gambler a very good Dalma portrait scroll to sell. In a few weeks he returned with a pouch of coins. In time they created a successful business. Then it suddenly stopped with Art Gambler owing Mad Monk an outstanding debt. Years later Mad Monk heard that Art Gambler had again started gambling with the gangs. He lost everything. He couldn't pay Mad Monk. He ran away. This time to a monastery up north.

"Oh well," shrugged Mad Monk in his studio, "another gallery bites the dust." With that Mad Monk painted Dalma contemplating the 'Varieties of Compulsions.' Including his own.

To show off his acquisitions in his new mansion a painting collector invited his like minded friends, local dignitaries and some well known artists to a party. Mad Monk didn't like these parties. He had to hold his tongue when he heard the boasting of other artists. Almost all of them tried to impress wealthy merchant art collectors, their wives and just as often their mistresses with stories about their new works and recent high priced sales.

Most of the artist monks attending the party were drinkers and partiers like Mad Monk. Plenty of wine, beer and food were set out on decorated tables. Cut flowers in intricate vases were placed next to exquisite old bonsai trees. It was a display of opulence as only The Rich can afford.

Unfortunately the artists were asked to wear their best monk suits. Perhaps because the homeowner wanted to show off how many famous monk artists he could get to his party.

Mad Monk thought, "The Rich are always competing to pay for and donate brilliant religious paintings, sculpture and shrines. Is this any way to fund a religion of abstinence, morality and inner truth?"

Mad Monk was standing by the wall watching the festivities when suddenly a voice he recognized asked, "How do you keep on painting 1000 Attitudes of Dalma? You turn them out like my wife makes 'kim chi,'" asked a collector that Head Monk had once brought to Mad Monk's studio. "Do you remember me?"

"Please tell me your name again," replied Mad Monk glibly, "I have a hard time remembering people who just stop in to look then don't buy my work."

"I'm called Skeptical Collector. I'd love to buy one of your paintings. But I've heard a rumor that you're not painting all of them. I've heard that you train your novices to paint in your exact style. How can I tell if a painting is yours or not?"

"What's the difference who painted it as long as it tells the viewer the story of Dalma's teachings?"

"Yes but that's only part of it. Each artist tells the story in his own way with certain subtleties of style. If I were to buy one of your paintings I want your visual version of Dalma's teachings. That's what I'm collecting. Not from an unknown novice who makes good copies."

"I don't know about novices painting my paintings. I can tell you where my paintings come from. They come from walking the way, meeting people, helping them if I can. I don't copy any other painters. Dalma's Spirit directs my hands when I paint. I don't deliberately use my style, it uses me. Whoever is spreading this rumor needs attention badly. I won't give it any."

"Then answer me this Mad Monk, where does your Dalma Spirit come from. Where does it live? If it's real why can't I see it or feel it? It must have a source because all things have a source."

"Imagination has no need of a source," replied Mad Monk patiently, "It's anywhere and everywhere waiting for people to use it. Some do, some don't, some can't. It's like air. You can't see it but you can feel its hot and cold winds."

"In your lifetime will you meet enough people so that you can paint 1000 Attitudes of Dalma?" asked Skeptical Collector. "And if you're walking and meeting people all the time when do you have time to paint?"

"At the end of each day I paint what I have seen, heard and done on my journey on the way. Will I paint more than 1000 Attitudes? Yes if each day is like this one. Could happen."

"I don't believe there are that many interesting people in the world," said Skeptical Collector, "I've been told I'm one of the most interesting people anyone's ever met. Why don't you paint me as an Attitude?"

With that Mad Monk tapped his head, walked away from Skeptical Collector. He joined in a boring conversation about foreign art dealers and the problems communicating with them.

Late that night when he returned to his studio he painted Dalma contemplating, 'Exasperation from Egotistical Skeptics.'

ALWAYS SELLING

A wealthy, high society art collector named Always Selling came to visit Mad Monk's studio. They cordially greeted when he entered. Always Selling looked with a practiced eye at each scroll as Mad Monk unrolled then hung them on wall hooks. Mad Monk urgently thought, "I've shown you all the best ones. Buy one or two. I haven't made a substantial donation to the monastery in a few months."

Always Selling didn't say a word until, "Mad Monk you are an unsung master of the art of Dalma portraits. I want to make you famous. That means many more people will come to you to buy. Here's what I want to do. You will paint one of your masterpieces on my wife's formal kimono. In fact later today I'm buying her a new kimono made of the finest silk. She will wear it to the best parties and political events. We know many important people. It will be a beautiful thing. Your art will be there with her for all to see."

Mad Monk looked at Always Selling. "I'm an ink and brush painter. I've never painted on a silk kimono. I will have to do some experiments. Kindly leave me some money for the paints and fabrics. I'll let you know what I learn." Always Selling looked at Mad Monk with surprise, "I'm not going to pay you for experiments. I'm not going to pay you for anything. I'm offering you a grand introduction into high society. These are people who buy paintings. They will see your painting on her kimono. They will talk about it. They will decide they too must have one. Besides my wife is famous as a fashion leader. This is very good for your career. Suddenly you will be known throughout the Empire. People will ask 'who painted Dalma's portrait on your fabulous kimono? We will answer 'why of course everyone knows the one and only Mad Monk whose studio is at the San shin Mountain monastery.'"

"I would love to do this for you," replied Mad Monk, "but I can't. I could never satisfy the demand that your wife's kimono will create. I don't paint on command. I paint when Dalma reveals one of his 1000 Attitudes to me. Also I'm not so sure I want to promote myself on a rich woman's back. That's different than a painting. There are designers who can do that."

Always Selling retorted, "You sir have no right to call yourself an artist. I think you're selfish. You only want to keep your work for yourself and your small group. You're an elitist."

Mad Monk thought for a moment then said, "You may be right. I do like my paintings. That's why I paint them. However I must get paid for my work. Yes I have a small group of collectors who support the monastery by buying my work. Can I ask for anything more?"

"You naïve Mad Monk are totally unaware of how the real world works," said Always Selling firmly, "you have to be out there with the people who can afford your art. Having your painting on my wife's kimono will get you into the best circles. Don't you want fame and fortune?"

"In that case wouldn't it be better," replied Mad Monk ruefully, "if I painted one of the 1000 Attitudes of Dalma on my own kimono. As far as circles, is any one circle better than another? I'm always walking where all kinds of people whether rich, middle class or poor see me. I walk in circles daily. That's how I get back here. Who better to talk about my work than me?

"If money and power are the differences in circles then it goes against our dedication to service. My paintings are about Dalma's teachings. They are part of the way and much more. Does your wife understand that? Do you?"

"I think I understand," said Always Selling, "Okay. I will pay you for a painting on my wife's kimono. But I have to see it first. If I like it you will be paid. If I don't then you missed a grand opportunity. I always get what I want."

"I can see you won't give up until I satisfy you. Come back tomorrow," said Mad Monk, "I will make you a special painting. If you like it I will learn how to transfer it."

Always Selling left Mad Monk's studio with a satisfied smile.

That night Mad Monk went to the village inn. While drinking he told his friends about the kimono offer. They all agreed it was a good thing as long as he was paid well and quickly. "We poor people can't let the rich take advantage of our skills. They never want to pay. That's how they get rich. Riding on our shoulders."

Late that night, just a little drunk Mad Monk went back to his studio. His paper, brushes and inks were on the table in front of him. Thinking about the kimono he started to paint. After he finished he fell into a deep satisfied sleep.

Always Selling returned next afternoon. Mad Monk said, "I made something specially for you. I hope you like it."

Mad Monk unrolled the scroll of paper. On it was a picture of Dalma with a very dissatisfied, confused look. He didn't look at all enlightened. In fact he looked as if he'd swallowed a snake.

"What's this?" Always Selling asked, "I expected a serene radiance. Not this horrible anguished look. What does this mean?"

"It's one of Dalma's 1000 Attitudes. This one is called the Attitude of 'Someone Who Always Wants Something for Nothing Even Though They Can Pay. When They Can't Get What They Want They Look Like They Swallowed A Snake.'"

"Not only are you disrespectful," exclaimed Always Selling haughtily, "you are also unenlightened. You live up to your reputation as the Mad Monk who says outrageous things for no reason at all."

"I don't think it's outrageous to tell the truth," smiled Mad Monk.

With that Always Selling left Mad Monk's studio leaving nothing behind but his part in the realization of one more of the 1000 Attitudes of Dalma.

Mad Monk sold that same painting at a good price to a friendly collector who revealed, "This reminds me of many of my business friends when they tell their stories of trying to get something for nothing from artists. I love it."

WALL GAZING

Head Monk walked into Mad Monk's studio accompanied by a well dressed stranger. "Mad Monk I want you to meet Rich and Powerful. He's an important art collector."

"I can speak for myself," said Rich and Powerful rudely interrupting, "Glad to meet you. I've heard a lot about you. I collect only the finest paintings that I keep in my mansions in the best parts of the best cities as well as in the mansions on my country estates where I have hundreds of laborers working to make sure there's food on the tables of our great country. I'd like to have several of your works for my collection. When can I expect them?"

"I have to think about it," said Mad Monk, "I'm planning a trip to the city to sell some small works for the monastery's building fund. I can start on your works in a few weeks."

"Forget about the trip to the city," said Head Monk, "Rich and Powerful has agreed to donate all the money we need for the building fund if he gets your pictures delivered within the week."

"I can't turn them out like a kitchen turns out meals," said Mad Monk, "my paintings take thought and time. I meditate on each one. What's the rush?'"

"The rush is," said Rich and Powerful, "I'm getting older every day. I'm going to retire soon to take up meditation, live the simple life, seek and attain enlightenment. I see it as the perfect end to my business career. Then I'll become a sage. I'm very goal centered. That's how I became rich. I never lose sight of what I want. Today one of my goals is to own several of your paintings."

"What kind of paintings are you seeking?" asked Mad Monk annoyed, "I specialize in portraits of Dalma."

"I want more than that. I want the ultimate, the finest, the greatest painting of the First Patriarch meditating. I want to see and feel him transcend into the Void through his No-Mind.

"When can you have the first one ready for me?" asked Rich and Powerful. "I'm having a party for some foreign business friends at my mountain mansion retreat near Seorak San. I want you to bring it up there for a grand unscrolling ceremony. You can stay as my guest to partake in the festivities. Please dress better than that. I expect you in seven days. Do not fail me."

Then the Head Monk and Rich and Powerful exited Mad Monk's studio.

Mad Monk instantly hated Rich and Powerful but couldn't show it because hatred goes against the Ten Zen Precepts. "Every painting I make is the ultimate one I can make at the time," thought Mad Monk, "I do have some ideas. Unfortunately I also feel the outrageous trickster Mad Monk awakening from his restful sleep. Hope I don't get into too much trouble."

Next morning the Head Monk came into Mad Monk's studio. "Just so you know," he paused, "I too dislike Rich and Powerful. However I bit the sword blade this time. We need the money. Kindly get him his painting in time so we can get our donation. And don't do anything to mess us up.

You understand don't you?"

"Yes sir," replied Mad Monk, "I will do the best I can do for all of us." A week later Mad Monk arrived at Rich and Powerful's stately mansion carrying the new scroll. Mad Monk was dazzled by the elegance. He thought, "All these expensive furnishings and paintings live here. Do these material obsessions know they are captives to their owner's enormous ego?"

Mad Monk was escorted into the main hall. A dozen well-dressed men were standing around holding silver cups talking animatedly to each other. Several traditionally dressed, incredibly beautiful women were sitting on couches covered in exquisite fabrics. Waiters walked around with 'ban chan' appetizers, sushi and sweets.

When Rich and Powerful saw Mad Monk he rushed up to him. "I've been waiting for you. Is that it? Is that it?" he excitedly asked Mad Monk.

"Yes, it's yours now. Enjoy it," said Mad Monk handing him the scroll.

"Everyone!" Rich and Powerful exclaimed loudly, "Stop! Look! And listen! Here's the painting I told you about. This is the finest painting of Dalma Meditating by our most famous living painter Mad Monk. I'm going to unroll the scroll in a moment. But first I'd like to ask the ambassador from Fredonia to help me."

The ambassador came forward. Rich and Powerful instructed him to take the other end of the rolled scroll hand waxed dowel. Then together they pulled the silk chord tying it. It unfurled, dropped down, now exposed to the assembled guests. Suddenly there's a hush. Not a sound. Everyone stared except Rich and Powerful who beamed in his glory. Within moments he realized something was wrong. He asked a waiter to hold his end of the scroll. He then walked around in front to take a look.

What he saw was a painting of an anonymous dirty wall. Just a grey wall not even recently painted. There were beautifully painted blemishes, cracks and age spots.

"What is this?" Rich and Powerful demanded loudly, "Some kind of Mad Monk joke? Where is the real Dalma painting? Mad Monk explain this now or get out without any donation."

"This is one of my most serious paintings," began Mad Monk, "It's the very wall Dalma stared at during his nine years of wall gazing meditation in Loyong. It's this common wall that inspired him to create his revered sutra sermon Lankavatara. It instructs us not to rely on words or images. Instead to point our seeking selves directly to our own Minds. To see into our own true inner Nature. To see ourselves as we really are. If you meditate on this wall you too will achieve enlightenment as did the First Patriarch."

"But I wanted a portrait. Look around. I have walls. Lots of walls," said Rich and Powerful in a complaining tone.

"Yes, we all have walls. But not this wall. This is Dalma's Wall. I walked to Mt Sung monastery near Loyong to see the genuine wall for myself. I came back a different man. You are the only human who will have this wall in his mansion. It's better than a portrait. Anyone can have a portrait. This wall is a portrait of the Mind of Dalma the Ultimate 'Sunim' Master. Tomorrow you will sit in front of it for meditation. Then you'll know you're on your way to enlightenment."

Suddenly a voice was heard from the crowd, "If you don't want 'Sunim' Mad Monk's painting I'll buy it from you right now," said Head Monk. "Even we at the monastery don't have a magnificent "Dalma's Wall." It will inspire all our monks to meditate with their absolute purist minds."

"No! Never!" roared Rich and Powerful. "If you, learned Head Monk want it then it's the real thing. I will hang it in my meditation room. I will take it with me everywhere. Better yet I want six more just like it for my other mansions. Mad Monk, I will pay you handsomely for them and still donate my money to the monastery's building fund. Soon as possible."

Rich and Powerful turned to his guests declaring, "You can all see it now. I'm on the road to enlightenment. I have Dalma's Wall."

"Yes you are," said Mad Monk, "more than any other rich man. You are now like Dalma. A prince who inspired the world."

Suddenly there came a cry from the crowd. "I want a wall painting as soon as possible," demanded one guest."

"I want one first," exclaimed another firmly.

"Me first. I'll pay more than anyone."

"Me too!"

"Don't forget about me. I already meditate."

Then Rich and Powerful spoke, "My friends, I must have the only wall painting. I'm the next Dalma. I'm The Prince. Me. Not any of you. Me!"

Mad Monk and Head Monk left the arguing dignitaries and merchants. On their way back to the monastery they talked about ideas for wall paintings that would entice donations from rich merchants seeking enlightenment.

"I still don't like Rich and Powerful," remarked Mad Monk. "He will never attain enlightenment. At his age his ego won't let him. Even if he completely changes his life."

"Yes I know, but in reality" said Head Monk. "monasteries are built from the spiritual desires of rich men. Not from sincere old ladies' weekly tithes."

"Any experienced house painter can make a decent Dalma wall painting," said Mad Monk, "I can't. More 1000 Attitudes of Dalma await me on the way."

"Go, finish them and be blessed in Heaven," opined Head Monk, "Meanwhile I will find wall painters for you to employ in your new studio annex. I can see them now: From the studio of Mad Monk. We won't starve this winter."

With that Mad Monk tapped his forehead and ran away. When Mad Monk returned to his studio he painted Dalma contemplating 'Walls Can Keep Enlightenment In and Out.'

PATHS TO CHARITY

Mad Monk was invited to a birthday dinner for Head Monk. When he arrived in the Assembly Hall many dignified older monks and Temple supporters sat at a very large square table.

Each guest could see all the others. Several bottles of the finest 'soju' wine from Andong Province were placed on the table. In the traditional manner they took turns pouring the precious liquor into each other's beautifully handcrafted ceramic cups.

Shortly a traditional meal began with several dozen 'ban chan' small dishes served by the traditionally attired hostess and her waitresses. An entranced young woman played well known and abstract melodies on her 'kayageum' floor lute. Another sang traditional Korean songs about mystical mountains, the all healing sun, magical stars, inspirational moons, wise shamans and their pet tigers, mysteries of life and of course the eternal spiritual family.

When the table was cleared except for wine, sweets and fresh fruits each guest told a story, a joke or sang a well known song with a drunken lilt. When it was Mad Monk's turn he stood up with a small rolled up scroll in his hand. He unrolled it then showed it around the room. The friends of the Head Monk nodded in agreement. They loved this new portrait of their friend and mentor.

"This is painted with strong memories of you in my brush. I will do another one in twenty years so you must take good care of yourself. And us." Everyone applauded.

Then Mad Monk took another small scroll from his bag. Unrolled it showed a portrait of Dalma holding a 'foo gwa,' bitter melon. "This is my donation for the Temple. It is Dalma contemplating 'Bitterness Is Also Health.'"

Everyone laughed at the irony. Head Monk received the scrolls with gracious bows. He then called over their hostess. He handed her 'Dalma with Bitter Melon.' "This is for you," he said, "Any one of the Mad Monk's paintings are valuable treasures. This will pay for tonight's superb heaven inspired feast."

Then Head Monk looked around the table. "Now I will donate this portrait of me to our Temple's Orphanage. If the nuns run out of money they can sell it to one of you." Everyone nodded in smiling agreement.

When the Mad Monk returned to his studio he painted Dalma contemplating 'Charity Needs Many Journeys.'

WEALTHY PRINCESS

Perhaps because Mad Monk was a well known and admired painter of 1000 Attitudes of Dalma, he was invited to a party at a Wealthy Princess's summer mansion. Mad Monk had heard from Head Monk that she too was an artist.

When he arrived entrance guards ushered him into in her studio. Everyone was looking at her newest series of paintings titled, "1000 Shades of Dalma's Big Toenail." Mad Monk looked too. For some incomprehensible to him reason they were each painted with different colors, hues, and glosses in precisely separated stripes. There were too many too close.

Mad Monk was standing there pondering in disbelief the totality of this abstract display of meaningless colorations when he heard someone say, "I've heard she spends fortunes having exclusive colors made just for her. She won't tell anyone where she gets them or who mixes them. There are rumors that she has the plant and mushroom color mixers killed after they deliver. There's no proof of course. I want to believe these ignorant foragers are sworn to silence. Mountain people know how to stay closed mouth if they're paid well. But her enemies persist. People love to gossip about Wealthy Princesses."

When Mad Monk heard these comments, his mind began to boil. He was enraged at the thought of someone killing poor mountain foragers and color mixers. He declared loudly, "Yes, lots of exotic colors here. What does it all mean? There's no profound insight. No inner nature revealed. It's not painting, it's cosmetology. Any toenail polisher can do the same."

Elegantly dressed people standing around him gasped in shocked horror. His words passed from mouth to mouth quickly reaching Wealthy Princess's bejeweled ears. She walked over to Mad Monk. Looking him in the eye she said, "As an artist you should know better than to mock another serious artist's work. I spend time and money creating beauty. People love my artwork. Now be nice. The art world has room for everyone."

"Time and money do not make an artist. We live in parallel art universes. Every so often they crash into each other. As long as there are Wealthy Princesses calling themselves artists I dare not call myself one."

She nearly choked from this new offense. "How dare you display your bad monastery manners in my home. You were only invited because I was told you are a famous painter. I thought we could be colleagues. We could talk about art. I was also told you are Mad Monk who makes outrageous comments. I was warned. I see you can't be trusted to behave yourself in decent company. You can leave now before I call my guards to throw you out."

"You mean the guards who are laughing behind your back? Truth be told I was already on my way out. Then I noticed the nail polishes on your guests. We all need inspiration from somewhere. I see that's yours. By the way, you shouldn't kill poor color mixers. They're trying to earn enough to feed their families."

"Guards!" she screamed.

Mad Monk tapped is forehead and said, "Thank you for enlightening me Wealthy Princess. I always wondered who makes those nail color paint charts in the beauty shops."

Then Mad Monk ran away back to his studio in the monastery. That night he painted a new attitude of Dalma contemplating 'Satisfaction from Fashionable Rejection' with black ink and brush.

Wealthy Princess never forgot nor forgave Mad Monk. Her guests never forgot either. Most nodded silent agreement with him.

Several years later Mad Monk heard a rumor that the Emperor ordered Wealthy Princess to stop painting. "You are making the upper classes look shallow," was his reason. Where could he have learned this, she wondered?

Mad Monk also heard that Wealthy Princess had hired a master jewelry maker to teach her the secret arts of lacquer, metallurgy and precious gems. It was also rumored that the jewelry master was creating and selling his jewelry with her name on it. That rumor couldn't be confirmed. The jewelry master died as soon as the rumors started.

WISDOM TO GO

While walking on the way Mad Monk saw a large neatly painted sign raised from the ground by two posts reading 'Wisdom To Go.' Stroking his beard he wondered what it meant. He looked at it carefully. It didn't point to anyplace. It didn't say where to go. He didn't see anyone near it.

He walked around the back of it. There he read another sign, 'Wisdom Has Gone. Follow. To the Inn."

Mad Monk tapped his forehead. He thought, "Signs along the way get in my way of observing Nature and helping humanity. Why would someone put them there?"

From then on he vowed to stop reading signs along the way. "Easier said then done," thought Mad Monk as he contemplated his day. "Perhaps I can read a book while walking. No, that defeats the purpose of walking along the way. The only thing for me to do is interpret those signs as inscrutable mystic messages from the other side of Mind. No matter what they're selling."

That night when Mad Monk returned to his studio he painted Dalma contemplating 'Ignoring Stupid Signs Along the Way.'

WALKING TO SILLY

While walking on the way Mad Monk walked by to an old monk walking with his head down clearly lost in thought. "Who are you and where are you going master 'sunim'?" asked Mad Monk respectfully. The old man jumped back. He stared at Mad Monk.

"You startled me. My name is Ageless Walker. I'm going nowhere. With neither direction nor destination. No past, present nor future captures me. I'm walking while meditating in alternative time. I do this to enjoy an ageless life," he replied.

Mad Monk's eyes widened. "I too would like to enjoy an ageless life. Can you teach me 'sunim'?"

"Ageless Walking is a teaching you must practice by yourself. You must walk without thinking. Walk until you don't think, can't think. Become a walking Mindless Mind. When you can do that you will be ageless. That is the whole of my longevity and health teaching. Many have tried. Those who live eternally don't talk about it," said Ageless Walker walking onward.

Everyday for many months Mad Monk tried walking without thinking. "Not as easy as it sounds," thought Mad Monk, "I cannot control the chattering monkeys in my too active head. I think about Dalma contemplating the universe, me climbing mountains, the beauty of trees on the way. I think about food, wine and women. I think about painting. I think about humanity. My conclusion is I'm not chosen to be ageless."

Mad Monk was about to give up ageless walking when he saw some children playing on the side of the road. Suddenly he had an idea for his own walking meditation. "If walking forward mindlessly can make one ageless," reasoned Mad Monk, "then walking backwards with a child's mind can help me grow younger."

Mad Monk began walking backwards, twisting his neck to see obstacles, often stumbling until he won his balance. Mad Monk loved walking backwards. He laughed like a child. He decided to walk backwards as much as he could.

A few weeks later while walking backwards Mad Monk again met Ageless Walker on the path. "Why are you walking backwards?" asked the old monk.

"I grow younger as I walk backwards," answered Mad Monk with a wild belly laugh.

"I see, " said Ageless Walker, "As you walk backwards you get sillier. Silliness is the essential pleasure and permanent attitude of eternal youth. I will walk backwards with you until I get silly. Thank you for this teaching."

"Yes, let's walk backwards like boys until our mother calls us home," said Mad Monk laughing.

So they walked backwards together, talking and laughing as children until they heard the monastery's commanding gong. Then they turned around running as fast as they could so they didn't miss their dinner.

After dinner Mad Monk went to his studio to paint Dalma contemplating 'Ageless Silliness.'

One fine day a woman from the city walked into Mad Monk's studio. "I'm People's Voice. I want to interview you for a book about artist's lives," she confidently stated. "Please tell me 'What Is Art?' in fifty words. Or less."

"Don't you know?" replied Mad Monk.

"I want your opinion," countered People's Voice.

"Can't you tell from my pictures?"

"Yes. And no. However I still want you to tell me. In your own words."

"What if I don't know?"

"You're an artist. You must have your own opinion. What is art?"

"Why is that your first question? What if I can't tell you? What if I've never thought about that question?" teased Mad Monk beginning to enjoy this conversation.

"Your answer will help me understand you. Artists are complex people."

"I'm not complex. I'm a simple monk working hard to support my monastery and Temple. Has nothing to do with what I think art is."

"Your fans want to know everything about you," she baited.

"What fans? I'm not an entertainer or court jester."

"You Sunim Master Mad Monk are a celebrity in our country and beyond. People love to see your paintings. Admit it or not people want to know about your life. And what you think."

"I can't imagine why," he responded, "I walk. I meet people. I try to make the world a better place. Painting 1000 Attitudes of Dalma is the thing I do instead of gardening."

"At last. Now we're getting somewhere. Art is gardening. You sow seeds, spread fertilizer, pray for rain, weed between plants, try to keep birds, bugs and pests out of your garden then wait for the rewards of a healthy crop. First time I heard that. Art is gardening."

"I didn't say art is gardening," retorted Mad Monk angrily, "I said I'm given dispensation to paint instead of spending my time in the monastery's garden. Head Monk knows his priorities. Anyone can have a successful garden with a little experience and luck."

"Are you saying anyone can make art given time and inspiration? What is inspiration?"

"I didn't say that. Painting is how I express what I see in the world of men and Nature meeting Dalma's teachings. The many ways to enlightenment. Complexity to simplicity. Confusion to clarity. Letting go of the mind's suffering from material desires and personal causes. Knowing one's own inner truth in alignment with Heaven. As above so below."

"Would you say art is the 1000 Attitudes of Dalma manifest in your paintings?" asked People's Voice.

"Yes if that will satisfy your curiosity. Now I have to get back to work."

"I have one more simple question. Do monks wear gray underwear?

"MU" Mad Monk shouted at her.

With that People's Voice ran out the door never to return.

Mad Monk was delighted she was gone. He laid down some paper, ground some ink, picked up his brush, sat at his desk and painted Dalma contemplating, 'Explaining the Unexplainable."

Occasionally Mad Monk wondered if his answer to the question "What is Art" was ever published. "If so," he pondered, "I hope I don't inspire all the gardener monks to become artists. We'll all starve."

END IT ALL

On a beautiful clear hot sunny day Mad Monk was walking on the way when he saw coming towards him a crazed looking young man in a very ragged, dirty long robe. He was carrying a sign on a bamboo pole that said: THE END IS COMING.

"Kindly stop for a moment young man," proposed Mad Monk in a cheery tone, "Who are you? Whose end is coming?"

"Not whose end!" said the ragged one feverishly, "Everyone and everything is coming to an end. My divinely channeled pre-apocalypse name is End It All."

"How can everything come to an end when everything is always changing? Everything is here one minute then gone the next. Everything's going towards it's own end. Everyone has a different everything. We only share a few things. Do you mean the end of the five elements? End of the Sun? End of Heaven? When is the end coming? Does anyone know for sure?"

"Don't ask me questions. Be afraid. Be scared. Be very afraid. Wake up and understand: The end is coming."

"Afraid of what?"

"Everything. Until the end comes," replied End It All.

"I am at peace with everything," said Mad Monk. "Everything changes all the time. I change but remain the same. The end is changing. The end comes and goes. Then what happens?"

"I don't know. It hasn't happened yet," End It All sheepishly shrugged.

"If you don't know when it's coming how do you know the end is coming?"

"I hear voices in my head that tell me the end is coming. I listen to them. They know things the rest of us don't know," replied End It All thoughtfully.

"Like what else? Besides the end coming?"

"They tell me to fast until I hear birds twitter divine messages. They tell me I'm a special person who has to warn everyone. Soon they promise to tell me how to save everyone. Soon as I get some food and drink," End It All said wearily.

Mad Monk dug into his shoulder bag, took out some coins, handed them to End It All who had a puzzled look. "The inn is straight ahead in the village," directed Mad Monk, "get yourself some food. You should take a bath and wash your clothes before the end. Don't want to be grubby and smelly when it happens, do you?"

"I'm afraid the innkeeper won't let me in the inn," countered End It All, "Kind monk would you go in and get me some food and drink. I'll eat my meal away from people on the edge of the village. I can't wash my robe. It holds my inner truth and memory. My robe has been with me since the voices. It knows things about the future."

Mad Monk thought for a long moment. "Come with me to the monastery. We have clothes, food and drink. We take care of wanderers on the way."

"No, sir monk I can't go to the monastery," replied End It All in a panic, "that's where my mission began. I too was a monk studying, meditating, gardening, doing everything monks do. Then one day while meditating I heard a voice say "The End Is Coming." I tried to ask it the same questions you asked me. All it would say was, "The End Is Coming." It started to drive me crazy. I went to Head Monk to ask him what to do. He told me, "In the far west over the great oceans monks and regular people hear the 'voice of the end' all the time. They put on long robes then walk the world carrying signs. The end hasn't come yet."

I turned in my monk's clothes for this long robe. I made this sign. I'm on my journey to The End. There's no going back. I must continue."

Mad Monk looked at End It All with some pity. "I've heard of monks driven mad from meditation discipline. Are you still meditating?"

"Of course. How else can I hear the voices? Each morning they tell me where to walk. They want their message spread far and wide. I will walk to the ends of this planet earth until The End. Then I will never walk again."

"My friend, I'm called Mad Monk because I don't follow the Precepts. I drink, fornicate with women, eat forbidden foods. Meeting you has made me think you also should be called Mad Monk. Not for the same reasons. But there can't be two of us. If you will let me paint your portrait in my studio I will be generous. It's just outside the monastery."

"As long as I don't have to go into the monastery."

"No problem. Come with me."

They walked to Mad Monk's studio. "Long as we're here I'll tell my novices to get us some food and tea. Please take off your robe and put on one that's there. Oh and before that let's go down to the river and bathe. We've both been walking in the hot sun all day. Take my extra towel with you."

When they returned from bathing, food was spread out. They ate and drank in silence. Then Mad Monk went to his painting table. He made ink in the ink stone, took out brushes from the bamboo holder, then painted Dalma contemplating the 'End Of It All.'

When he finished he showed End It All the painting. It was Divine Dalma with End It All's scared, fevered, frantic face.

"It one of the 1000 Attitudes of Dalma contemplating the 'Endless End Coming.' I also think Endless End is a better name for you."

"You may be right. Tomorrow when I meditate I will ask the voices if they approve."

"I'm sure they will," responded Mad Monk, "my own inner voices are also endless. They endlessly drive me to seek new ideas for paintings. It's why I walk and talk. May The End never arrive."

They toasted and drank until they slept.

HAPPY DEATH

Mad Monk was walking around the monastery courtyard talking to a young monk, "I have seen a truly happy death," he declared.

"How is that possible?" asked the young monk, "All deaths are sadly mourned by families and friends."

Mad Monk stopped to look at some flowers. "Listen to this story of a happy death. It started when a wealthy art gallerist invited me along with some of the best brush and ink painters in Korea to a lavish dinner. There was also as much foreign whiskey, soju and sake as we could drink.

"We were getting very drunk telling stories about our travels when suddenly the dinner table was removed from the room. We sat in our chairs staring at each other. Within a few moments a huge mulberry paper scroll was brought in then unrolled on the floor until it reached the far walls. And there was still more, much more unrolled awaiting our hands."

Then our host politely declared, "I invite each of you to take a turn painting whatever you wish. No limits." Our host clapped his hands. Servers brought in trays with brushes, ink, ink stones, water and towels.

"We painted all night," continued Mad Monk, "each taking his first turn and some more than one. The most famous and oldest of us was Yang Sun, from the southern Jiri San Mountains. He painted a version of his well known, much admired smiling Taoist shaman riding on the back of his fierce looking pet tiger. It showed great power.

"While watching the others paint the scroll we all drank and ate desserts. We were sitting and leaning wherever there was room. At 3am our host said, 'The time has come my talented friends. Please finish up whatever you're eating and drinking. Tonight I will let the scroll dry. Tomorrow I will cut it up into appropriate sections then display it in my gallery. Whatever money I get I will share with you.' We all agreed. What could we say?

"We were standing putting our coats on when someone went over to Yang Sun. He was sitting in a chair sleeping with his head down and his hands in his lap with a smile on his face. His name was called, getting louder with each demand to awaken.

"Someone went over and shook his shoulder. He softly fell over onto the floor. One of us was once a medic in the army. He came over and felt Yang Sun's neck. 'He's sleeping in painter's heaven from now on. Someone must call his family.'

"I remembered that Yang Sun told me he had no family. 'I've dedicated my life to painting. I live hidden in the mountains where no wife nor children would want to stay for long. Fellow painters, a few collectors and gallerists who make the journey to visit me, they are my family.'

"We didn't mourn him. We all wished, each and every one of us, that we should die the same way. With a smile like his glowing with satisfaction, wisdom and joy. I call his a happy death. Yang Sun was doing what he loved with people he loved doing it with. He will live eternally in our memories and imaginations."

"If only all of us could find a complete life commitment that would make us content and give us joy to the end," said the young monk.

With that Mad Monk tapped his forehead, ran to his studio to paint the Dalma contemplating 'Everyone's Truly Happy Ending.'

ACKNOWLEDGEMENTS

First in my heart, I couldn't have completed this book without the love, health care, literary and artistic support of Eleanor Heartney, my soul mate for the last 30 years. She nursed me through two major surgeries and my daunting recovery. She made many dozens of congee (rice soup) meals and varieties of vegan jellos from scratch using natural juices. She performed many other nursing chores that I won't describe because they're simply too disgusting. She watched me nap making sure I was still alive. She watched me during the phases of cardio rehab, endless walking our co-op hallways and climbing stairs. The human body in rebellion against life isn't a friendly or pretty sight. I thank her more than I can say.

I owe my Korean experiences and introduction to Jung-kwang Mad Monk to Nam June Paik, the philosopher/video/performance artist and Dr. Yongwoo Lee, Korean art critic, exhibition curator, GwangJu Art festival founder, Venice biennial Korean pavilion commissioner. Soon after a dinner party in New York where we talked about shamanism in art, Dr. Lee invited me to Korea for Nam June Paik's 60th birthday celebration. He commissioned me to write and read a critical work along with twenty other academics and arts writers invited for "Art 20/21 Festival and Conference" taking place in Seoul, South Korea at the same time as Paik's birthday gala. It was there that I premiered "Video Mudang" (Video Shaman) in front of 100 or so global art celebrities. Nam June Paik was, as he later said, awakened from academic torpor.

Paik's gallerist Holly Solomon, owner of the eponymous, successful and distinguished New York art gallery, asked me to repeat my performance in her space. It was vibrant and wild with hand played percussion. Within months I was accompanying Paik and team to the 1993 Venice Biennial performing "Video Mudang" (Video Shaman) with a Korean band at the opening of the award winning German pavilion. He was an influence and a mentor. I miss his bizarre takes on art and life. I'm sure he's entertaining and enlightening the multitudes in video heaven.

Wonsook Kim's relationship with Jung-kwang's artwork is especially satisfying for me. Her drawings embody the strength that art transcends all surface differences in cultures.

Finally, I applaud my friend Aldo Sampieri, artist and book designer who shared the struggle to get this book off our screens and into print. Without him this book wouldn't be the storytelling beauty it is.

Thank you all.

51271077R00078

Made in the USA
San Bernardino, CA
17 July 2017